# MORALITY, CULTURE, AND HISTORY

*Essays on German philosophy*

RAYMOND GEUSS

## CAMBRIDGE
UNIVERSITY PRESS

PUBLISHED BY THE PRESS SYNDICATE OF THE UNIVERSITY OF CAMBRIDGE
The Pitt Building, Trumpington Street, Cambridge CB2 1RP, United Kingdom

CAMBRIDGE UNIVERSITY PRESS
The Edinburgh Building, Cambridge CB2 2RU, UK
http://www.cup.cam.ac.uk
40 West 20th Street, New York, NY 10011-4211, USA    http://www.cup.org
10 Stamford Road, Oakleigh, Melbourne 3166 Australia

© Raymond Geuss 1999

First published 1999

Printed in the United States of America

*Typeface* Meridien 10/13 pt.    *System* MagnaType™ 3.52    [AG]

*A catalog record for this book is available from
the British Library*

*Library of Congress Cataloging-in-Publication Data*
Geuss, Raymond.
Morality, culture, and history : essays on German philosophy /
Raymond Geuss.
p.  cm.
Includes bibliographical references.
ISBN 0–521–63202–1 (hb). – ISBN 0–521–63568–3 (pbk.)
1. Philosophy, German – 20th century. 2. Philosophy, German – 19th
century. I. Title.
B3181.G48   1999
193 – dc21                    98-8083
CIP

ISBN 0 521 63202 1   hardback
0 521 63568 3   paperback

# CONTENTS

# PREFACE

IT isn't always appropriate to say, perhaps even to oneself, what one thinks and it certainly isn't appropriate to write down, much less to publish, everything one might in some contexts say. Anything one does write down will belong to some genre, and different genres impose different requirements. Each of the seven items in this collection was originally a separate essay and, despite the existence of some common themes and concerns, the volume is best read as a series of free-standing attempts to understand a set of overlapping but distinct philosophical and historical topics. Three of the essays have already been published and are reprinted without change: 'Nietzsche and Genealogy' and 'Nietzsche and Morality' appeared originally in *European Journal of Philosophy* (in volume 2, number 3, December 1994 and volume 5, number 1, April 1997, respectively), and 'Adorno and Berg' appeared as a chapter in *The Cambridge Companion to Berg* (edited by A. Pople, Cambridge 1996). 'Kultur, Bildung, Geist' first appeared in *History and Theory* (volume 35, number 2, 1996); the preparation of this volume gave me an opportunity to add some material to this essay, mostly in the form of additional footnotes, but I have not changed any of the basic claims or the basic structure. 'Equality and Equilibrium in the Ethics of Ernst Tugendhat' began life as a short contribution I wrote in German for a symposium on Ernst Tugendhat's book *Vorlesungen zur Ethik;* it was published in *Deutsche Zeitschrift für Philosophie* in volume 45 (1997) under the title *'Gleichheit und Gleichgewicht in der Ethik Ernst Tugendhats'.* In the course of translating the essay I found myself expanding what I had written in various ways, adding material, and shifting the focus increasingly from Tugendhat's views to various more general issues in ethics with the result that the English version printed here is now about twice the length of the original and contains a rather fuller discussion of some topics that were treated only in a very cursory way in the original essay. *'Art and Theodicy'* and *'Form and "the new" in Adorno's "Vers une musique informelle"'* are previously unpublished.

I count myself extremely lucky to have been able to move to Cambridge in 1993. This move has had a significant positive effect on my intellectual life and I'm indebted to a group of friends and colleagues here, mostly notably John Dunn, Geoff Hawthorn, Anna and István Hont, Susan James, Beverley and David Sedley, Quentin Skinner, and Michael Frede (Oxford), for their contribution to this effect.

I'm also very grateful to a number of people who have helped me in a variety of ways to put this volume together, especially to Drs Hilary Gaskin, Jeremy Mynott, and Onora O'Neill.

# 1

# NIETZSCHE AND GENEALOGY

IN 1971 Michel Foucault published an essay on Nietzsche's conception of 'genealogy'[1] and later began to use the term 'genealogy' to describe some of his own work.[2] Foucault's writings have been remarkably influential and so it wouldn't be at all odd for someone familiar with recent developments in history and the social sciences to come to think that Nietzsche had invented a new approach to these subjects called 'genealogy', an approach then further elaborated in the work of the late Foucault. It turns out, however, to be very difficult to say exactly what this new 'genealogical' form of inquiry is and how it is distinct from other approaches (if it is). A good way to go about trying to get clarity on this issue is, I think, to look with some care at Nietzsche's original discussion of 'genealogy'.

## I

Giving a 'genealogy' is for Nietzsche the exact reverse of what we might call 'tracing a pedigree'. The practice of tracing pedigrees is at least as old as the oldest Western literature. Thus Book II of the *Iliad* gives a pedigree of Agamemnon's sceptre:

Powerful Agamemnon
stood up holding the sceptre Hephaistos had wrought him carefully.
Hephaistos gave it to Zeus the king, son of Kronos,
and Zeus in turn gave it to the courier Argeiphontes,
and lord Hermes gave it to Pelops, driver of horses,
and Pelops gave it to Atreus, the shepherd of the people.
Atreus dying left it to Thyestes of the rich flocks,

and Thyestes left it in turn to Agamemnon to carry
and to be lord over many islands and over all Argos.
Leaning upon this sceptre he spoke . . .[3]

   This early example exhibits the main features of what I will
call a 'pedigree'. The general context is one of legitimizing or at
any rate of positively valorizing some (usually contemporary)
person, institution, or thing. That he has inherited such an
ancestral sceptre gives Agamemnon's words an extra weight
and constitutes a kind of warrant to be lord over 'Argos' and
'many islands'. The authority this sceptre gives Agamemnon –
to speak anachronistically, the Greeks having notoriously had
no word for 'authority' – is generally accepted by the other
figures who appear in the *Iliad*. In fact that is in some sense the
whole problem because, as Diomedes acidly remarks at the
beginning of Book IX, although Zeus did give Agamemnon the
sceptre 'he did not give you a heart, and of all power this is the
greatest' (IX.39). The only two instances we are given of explicit resistance to this authority are Achilleus and Thersites.
Odysseus makes a characteristically utilitarian use of Agamemnon's sceptre to beat Thersites into submission (II.265ff.),[4] but
Achilleus is not amenable either to the pedigree or the physical
weight of the sceptre.[5]

   The pedigree of the sceptre traces Agamemnon's possession
of it back through a series of unbroken steps of transmission to
a singular origin. For the pedigree actually to discharge its function the origin to which it recurs must be an actual source of
positive value, and each of the steps in the succession must be
value-preserving. So in the case of this particular pedigree it is
important that one can trace the ownership of the sceptre back
to Hephaistos and Zeus, the former presumably guaranteeing
the quality of the workmanship, the latter the associated claim
to political authority, and it is equally important that each step
in the transmission is a voluntary donation.[6]

   This kind of pedigree, then, has five main characteristics:

1. In the interests of a positive valorization of some item
2. the pedigree, starting from a singular origin
3. which is an actual source of that value
4. traces an unbroken line of succession from the origin to that item
5. by a series of steps that preserve whatever value is in question.

One might think that this way of thinking (and especially characteristic 5) overlooks an important feature of pedigrees, namely that in certain cases the longer the pedigree – the further back it can be traced – the better, the greater the resultant valorization. A family that could trace its patent of nobility back to the 15th century might think that this pedigree showed it to be more noble than a family whose patent went back only to the 19th century. Two distinct thoughts run together in this. First, that what is older is better, i.e. a more genuine or more intense source of value, so that getting into contact with it is inherently desirable and it is just an accident that getting in touch with this source of value requires a large number of steps of succession. The second thought is that the increasing number of steps – the passage of time itself – enhances the prestige or value of the item in question: It isn't that the older is necessarily a better *source* of value than what is more recent, but the value increases through succession. This suggests that one should perhaps revise 5 to read:

5\*. by a series of steps that preserve or enhance whatever value is in question.

'Genealogy' as practiced by Nietzsche differs from the tracing of a pedigree in all five respects. 'Genealogy' is certainly not undertaken with the intention of legitimizing any present person, practice, or institution, and won't in general have the effect of enhancing the standing of any contemporary item. As

far as points 2 and 3 are concerned, genealogy doesn't characteristically discover a single origin for the object of its investigation. To take the example Nietzsche himself analyzes in greatest
detail, Christian morality does not go back to a single instituting
activity by a particular person or small group in ancient Pal-
estine. The whole point of *Genealogy of Morality* is that Christian
morality results from a conjunction of a number of *diverse* lines
of development: the *ressentiment* of slaves directed against their
masters (*GM* I.1–10), a psychological connection between
'having debts' and 'suffering pain' that gets established in archaic commercial transactions (*GM* II.4–6), a need people come
to have to turn their aggression against themselves which results from urbanization (*GM* II.16), a certain desire on the part
of a priestly caste to exercise dominion over others (*GM* III.16)
etc.[7] The genealogy reveals Christian morality to arise from the
historically contingent conjunction of a large number of such
*separate* series of processes that ramify the further back one goes
and present no obvious or natural single stopping place that
could be designated 'the origin'.[8]

Furthermore, the further back the genealogy reaches the
less likely it is to locate anything that has unequivocal, inherent
'positive' value which it could transmit 'down' the genealogical
line to the present.[9] When Nietzsche writes that our world of
moral concepts has an origin ('*Anfang*') which 'like the origin
('*Anfang*') of everything great on earth, was for a long time and
thoroughly doused in blood' (*GM* II.6) he is opposing the sentimental assumption that things we now value (for whatever
reason) *must* have had an origin of which we would also ap-
prove.[10] Nietzsche thinks that this unquestioned assumption
has tacitly guided much historiography and constitutes both an
obstacle to understanding and a symptom of debility. Nietzsche,
of course, is not committed to the 'world of moral concepts'
that comprises 'duty', 'guilt', 'conscience' and such things any-
way, and that this world had its origins in blood and cruelty is
no argument against it for him (although it might be an ar-

4

gument against it for those who hold the sentimental view mentioned above). Equally the violent and bloody origins of Christian morality is for Nietzsche no argument *in favour* of it.[11] Value-preserving (or value-enhancing) transmission is perhaps a slightly more complex phenomenon than the origination of value because very different kinds of transfer might be recognized: Agamemnon's sceptre could be legitimately passed on by donation *inter vivos* or testament. However 'value-preserving transmission' is understood in a given pedigree, Nietzsche seems to go out of his way to emphasize that the history delineated in a genealogy won't generally exhibit unbroken lines of value-preserving succession, but will rather be characterized by an overwhelming contingency, and dominated by violent forms of human action based on pervasive delusions. Thus the origin of 'bad conscience' was 'not a gradual, not a voluntary transformation' nor was it 'an organic growing-over-into new conditions' but rather was 'a break, a leap, a coercion' (*GM* II.17). It seems reasonable, then, to assume that a genealogy won't exhibit characteristics 4 and 5 of a pedigree.

II

I lay such great stress on the difference between tracing a pedigree and giving a genealogy because the difference seems to me often overlooked with the result that Nietzsche comes to be seen as a conscious archaizer like Ludwig Klages or Heidegger. Thus Habermas misses the distinction and ends up attributing to Nietzsche just about the exact reverse of the position he actually holds:

> . . . Nietzsche has recourse to . . . the myth of origins . . . : the *older* is that which is *earlier* in the chain of generations, that which is nearer to the origin (*Ursprung*). The *more aboriginal* (*das Ursprünglichere*) has standing as that which ought to be more revered, that which is nobler, less corrupt, purer, in short: better.

5

Descent (*Abstammung*) and origin (*Herkunft*) serve as the criterion of rank in both a social and a logical sense.[12]

Habermas is right to emphasize the importance of 'rank' and
'rank-ordering' in Nietzsche. Nietzsche is a conscious radical
anti-egalitarian not just in politics[13] but also in ethics. He explicitly rejects the view that there should be one morality for
everyone (*JGB* §§198, 43, 30). In fact he even holds that it is
'*immoral*' to apply the principle 'What is fair for one person, is
fair for another' (*JGB* §221). Morality is to be subordinated to
the principle of rank-ordering (*JGB* §§221, 219, 228, 257).
Habermas is wrong, however, to connect this line of argument
with a purported greater nobility of that which is older or more
aboriginal.

Habermas also attributes to Nietzsche a 'pragmatist theory of
cognition' and a view of truth which 'reduces' it to preference.[14] I'm skeptical of this attribution; there is at any rate a
clear and strong strand in Nietzsche's published works that explicitly contrasts 'what is true' and what anyone might prefer,
desire or find useful. I would like now to consider some passages that exhibit this strand:

At *FW* §344 Nietzsche is discussing the belief he thinks con-
stitutive of 'science', namely that truth is more important than
anything else. This belief could not have arisen from a 'calculation of usefulness' because 'truth *and* untruth both continuously show themselves to be useful'.[15] If that is the case,
'usefulness' can't be the criterion by which truth is distinguished from untruth, and it becomes difficult to see how this
passage would be compatible with a pragmatist theory of truth
or cognition.

At *JGB* §39 Nietzsche claims that something might be true
even though it is 'in the highest degree harmful and dangerous'; it might be a basic property of existence that full cognition
of it would be fatal. I assume that the 'truth' at issue here is the
metaphysical truth that human existence is at best an insignifi-

cant tissue of senseless suffering. We might not be inclined to think of this as an archetypical 'truth', but Nietzsche was.[16] Here, too, it is hard to see how one could reduce this 'truth' to any kind of preference.

At *JGB* §120 Nietzsche speaks of the 'philosophers of the future' (with, it seems to me, evident approval) and reports that they will smile if anyone says to them: 'That thought exalts me; how could it not be true?' They won't be inclined to believe that truth will be pleasing to them.

At *GM* I.1 Nietzsche 'wishes' that the English psychologists who are his main opponents might be generous-spirited, courageous, and proud animals who have trained themselves 'to sacrifice all that they wish were the case to the truth'.

No one of these examples is perhaps decisive but the cumulative effect is, I think, to make one suspicious of attributing to Nietzsche any very straightforward kind of pragmatist theory of truth or any view that directly reduces truth to mere preference. This suspicion should be reinforced by a careful reading of *GM* III.24–25, where Nietzsche presents it as one of his main philosophical achievements to have called into question the value of truth (and of the will-to-truth).[17] For a pragmatist there isn't really much point in 'calling into question' the value of truth. The value of truth is obvious; after all, for the pragmatist we just *mean* by 'truth' what works, and how could that *not* have value for us?[18] Similarly if truth is just a matter of preference, the will-to-truth is unproblematic and doesn't need, one would think, any special 'justification': If 'the truth' can turn out to be something *contrary* to what I would prefer to believe, then I might ask why I should nevertheless pursue it (have a 'will-to' it) but surely I don't need some special justification to have a will-to-'what-I-prefer'. The kind of detailed and often subtle accounts Nietzsche gives of the various different ways truth (and untruth) have (or lack) values of different kinds, are pleasing to us (or not), conform to what we would wish or prefer to be the case (or not), make most sense if one assumes that Nietzsche takes truth, preference and value to be *prima facie* distinct things and does not have a philosophically reductive account which would settle the matter from the start on general grounds and make detailed investigation otiose. From the fact that Nietzsche does not seek to 'reduce' (in the sense in which philosophers use that term) truth to preference, utility, taste etc. it does not, of course, follow that it is not of great importance to investigate the multiple way in which claims to truth are connected with various value-judgments.

Nietzsche does wish to criticize the correspondence theory of truth and the unquestioned belief in the absolute value of truth, but he does not try to substitute his own 'theory' of truth for the correspondence-theory. If one takes a basically Platonist view (to the effect that one must begin by asking and answering the question: 'What is . . . (truth)?') it will seem that there is a huge gap or blank at what ought to be the centre of Nietzsche's philosophy, and one will be strongly tempted to fill in the blank: If Nietzsche clearly attacks the correspondence view, shows no interest in coherence, and seems to present no clear alternative of his own invention, then he must tacitly hold some kind of reductivist or pragmatist view. The most fruitful way of taking Nietzsche seems to me to see him not as trying to propound his own variant theory of truth, but as formulating a new question 'How and why does the will-to-truth come about?' (and claiming that this question is more interesting than, and doesn't presuppose an antecedent answer to Plato's question 'What is truth?').

Finally it is in some sense correct, as Habermas claims, that Nietzsche wishes to 'enthrone *taste* . . . as the only organ of a "cognition" beyond true and false, good and evil'.[19] However if, as I have suggested above, the elevation of the faculty of taste is not associated with a 'reduction' of truth claims to mere claims of subjective preference, there is no reason to believe that this increased standing for taste need imply, as Habermas thinks it does, that 'contradiction and critique lose their sense'.[20] Taste may in fact be held to be more important than truth and yet it not be the case that I can reject certain statements *as untrue because* they don't appeal to me.

### III

Having cleared away some of the debris blocking access to Nietzsche's texts, we can turn our attention to what he says about 'genealogy'.

Much of Nietzsche's later work is devoted to trying to give a 'genealogy' of Christianity and its associated ascetic morality, and so this genealogy of Christianity seems a reasonable place to start.

Like many other religions, 'Christianity' has a bi-partite structure: a set of antecedently existing practices, modes of behaviour, perception, and feeling which at a certain time are given an interpretation which imposes on them a meaning they did not have before[21] (*FW* §353). Thus in the specific case of Christianity Nietzsche distinguishes: a) a way of life or 'practice' which is specifically associated with Jesus because he is thought to have instantiated it to a particularly high degree and in a particularly striking way, but which is in principle livable almost anywhere and at any time (*A* §39, *WM* §212) – a form of life, i.e. of instinctive practice, *not* a form of belief, which consists in the unconditional forgiveness of enemies, failure to resist evil, abstention from use of force or the moral condemnation of others, etc. (*A* §§33, 35, 39, *WM* §§158–163, 211–212) – from b) a particular interpretation put on that way of life (as instantiated by Jesus), i.e. a set of propositions that eventually become the content of Christian belief/faith. This interpretation is more or less 'invented' by Paul (*A* §42) and contains various dogmatic propositions about the existence of God, the immortality of the soul, human sinfulness and need for redemption etc. (*A* §§39–43, *WM* §§167–171, 175, 213). Paul did succeed in getting his reading of the 'meaning' of Jesus' life

accepted but his dogmas did not fit very comfortably with the
original form of practice Jesus instantiated. To be more exact,
Paul's 'interpretation' represents so drastic and crude a misinterpretation of Jesus' way of life that even at a distance of 2000
years we can see that wherever the Pauline reading gets the
upper hand – and it has in general *had* the upper hand for most
of the period in question – it transforms 'Christianity' (as we
can now call the amalgam of Jesus' form of life and Paul's
interpretation of it) into what is the exact reverse of anything
Jesus himself would have practiced. An essentially apolitical,
pacifist, non-moralizing form of existence (cf. *WM* §207) is
transformed into a 'Church', a hierarchically organized public
institution, 'just the thing Jesus preached against' (*WM* §168,
cf. *WM* §213).

Paul's interpretation of Jesus' life (which forms the core of
what will eventually become 'Christian theology') is wrong in
two ways. First of all it is a misunderstanding of Jesus' way of
life. For Paul Jesus' life and death essentially has to do with sin,
guilt and redemption, but the message of Jesus' life really is that
there *is* no 'sin' (*A* §33), that the very concept of 'guilt' is
'abolished' (*A* §41). Second, Paul's propositional beliefs, taken
by themselves (and not as a purported 'interpretation' of the
meaning of Jesus' practice) are false. For Nietzsche the whole
notion of 'sin' is in its origin a priestly misinterpretation of
certain physiological states of debility and suffering (*GM* III.16–
17, III.20) and the concept 'guilt' in the full-blown Christian
sense depends on the false assumption that humans have freedom of the will and can thus decide to exercise or refrain from
exercising the various powers they have (*GM* I.13, *M* §112, *JGB*
§§18, 21, *GM* III.15, 20).

Paul's hijacking of the form of life embodied by Jesus is one
episode in what Nietzsche calls the 'genuine history' of Christianity (*A* §39), but it shows with particular clarity the bi-
partite structure (of 'form of life' on the one hand and 'interpretation' on the other) which was mentioned earlier. It is

important to see that Paul's (successful) attempt to take over the Christian form of life by reinterpreting it is only the first of a series of such episodes (*WM* §214, cf. *GM* II.12–13). Each such event can be described as at the same time a new interpretation of Christianity-as-it-exists (at the given time) *and* as an attempt to take over or get mastery of that existing form of Christianity.[22] Each historically successive interpretation/*coup de main* gives the existing Christian way of life a new 'meaning'. Although Nietzsche at one point says that Paul 'annuls original Christianity' (*'das ursprüngliche Christentum'*) (*WM* §167), this doesn't mean that Paul wishes to abolish wholesale the practices that constitute this primordial form of Christianity. Rather he wants to impress on them the stamp of a certain meaning, give them a certain direction. Nietzsche thinks that such attempts to take over/reinterpret an existing set of practices or way of life will not in general be so fully successful that *nothing* of the original form of life remains, hence the continuing tension in post-Pauline Christianity between forms of acting, feeling, judging which still somehow eventually derive from aboriginal Christianity and Paul's theological dogmas. Equally once Paul's reading of Christian practice has given these practices a certain 'meaning' the historically *next* re-interpretation will in turn find the Pauline meanings already embedded in the form of life it confronts and will be unlikely in giving a new interpretation of that form of life to be able to abolish Pauline concepts and interpretations altogether. Historically, then, successive layers of such 'meanings' will be, as it were, deposited (*GM* II.13). There will be some gradual change in the actual practices and form of life – Pauline Christianity will begin to develop a Church organization which primordial Christianity didn't have – and a rather more mercurial shift in the dominant 'interpretation' given to the practice, but even the dominant interpretation won't have been able utterly to eradicate the 'meanings' that have previously accumulated, i.e. that have been imposed upon 'Christianity' by a series of past agencies.

11

I write 'agencies' advisedly because although I have up to now focused on an episode in which a particular individual (Paul) reinterpreted/attempted-to-get-mastery of an existing form of life, it need not be a particular human individual (i.e. a biologically singular animal) who is the agent. According to Nietzsche, one can perfectly well speak of 'The Church' trying to get control of, and impose an interpretation on certain ways of living, feeling and acting, such as for instance the various mendicant movements that arose at the end of the medieval period. In fact in this context Nietzsche doesn't speak of 'agencies' as I have, but of 'wills'. Nietzsche uses the term 'will' in a very flexible and expansive way to refer both to smaller and to larger entities than the will of a biologically individual human being. One can, according to Nietzsche, look at what we would normally call 'my will' as a kind of resultant of the struggle within me of various drives, impulses, and desires, and each of these can itself in some sense be called a 'will'. Similarly one can attribute a 'will' to various entities that are larger than me: The University of Cambridge can have a will, so can the UK, the European Union, etc.

The history of Christianity, then, is a history of successive attempts on the part of a variety of different 'wills' to take control of and reinterpret a complex of habits, feelings, ways of perceiving and acting, thereby imposing on this complex a 'meaning'. Although the 'meaning' imposed at any time by a successful will may in some sense be superseded by a later 'meaning' (imposed by a later will), the original meaning will in general not go out of existence altogether but will remain embedded in at least a modified form in the complex we call 'Christianity'. Part of the reason for this is that once a certain will has been able to impose its meaning on Christianity, it acquires a certain power of resistance to any further attempts on the part of *other* wills to impose their meaning on the Christian complex. Once Pauline theology has penetrated Christian practice, modified it, given it a certain direction and a particular kind of coherence, etc., any non-Pauline will which tries to impose a *new* interpretation on Christianity (as thus constituted) won't encounter, as it were, just a tabula rasa, but a set of actively structured forces, practices etc. which will be capable of active resistance to attempts to turn them into other directions, impose new functions on them etc. So each episode of 'reinterpretation' will be a struggle between a will impinging from without bent on mastery/imposition-of-a-new-meaning and a complex way of life which will resist at least by inertia and evasion and probably by more active measures.

Christianity at a given point in time will be a 'synthesis' of the various different 'meanings' imposed on it in the past and which have succeeded in remaining embedded in Christian feeling, forms of action and belief, etc. There will be nothing necessary or even particularly coherent about such a 'synthesis': What 'meanings' it will contain and how they will be related to each other will be just the result of history, and this history will be contingent in a number of ways. It will be contingent which wills encounter and try to 'interpret'/master Christianity at what times and under what circumstances, and it will be contingent how much force, energy, and success they will have in imposing their 'meaning'.[23] The history of Christianity will 'crystallize itself into a kind of unity which is difficult to dissolve, difficult to analyse, and, it must be emphasized, utterly *undefinable*' (*GM* II.13).

One can't give a 'definition' of Christianity *if* one means by that an account of a purported essential meaning (or purpose or function) which is invariably characteristic of Christianity. 'Only that which has no history is definable' (*GM* II.13) because anything that has a history will partake, like Christianity, in the continuing struggle between wills attempting to impose their meaning or purpose on the item in question, a struggle with constantly shifting outcomes. Instead of a 'definition' one must try to give an 'analysis' of the contingent synthesis of 'meaning' Christianity (for instance) represents. This process of disentangling the separate strands will take the form of a historical account. The reason for this seems to be that 'at an earlier stage that synthesis of "meanings" presents itself in such a way as to be more easily dissolved' (*GM* II.13), that is, at an earlier stage the individual elements are more distinct.

The appropriate historical account is a genealogy. Starting from the present state of, say, Christianity (or of whatever else is the object of genealogical analysis), the genealogy works its way backward in time, recounting the episodes of struggle between different wills, each trying to impose its interpretation or meaning on the Christianity that existed at its time, and thereby disentangling the separate strands of meaning that have come together in a (contingent) unity in the present. Each such episode is, as it were, the branching node of a genealogical tree (see figure on page 15).

This diagram is intentionally just a sketch of Nietzsche's account, leaving out many details in order to exhibit more clearly the overall structure. At various points the branches simply end (e.g. with the 'grammatical distinction between subject and predicate' on the right toward the top) but those end-points are not absolute origins. The genealogy peters out there either because there is no more information available or because further elaboration of the genealogy at that point would lead too far afield, but in principle if information were available and there were any *reason* to continue, one could carry on with the genealogy back behind any of the points at which Nietzsche in fact stops.

This is true in particular for the end-point I have designated 'Jesus' radically non-moralizing form of life'. I said at the beginning of this discussion (p. 9) above) that religions for Nietzsche generally had a bi-partite form: a particular way of behaving or living on the one hand and a particular interpretation of that way of living on the other. In this case, there is Jesus' way of life and Paul's interpretation of it, and only both *together* constitute what we call 'Christianity'. One might think that

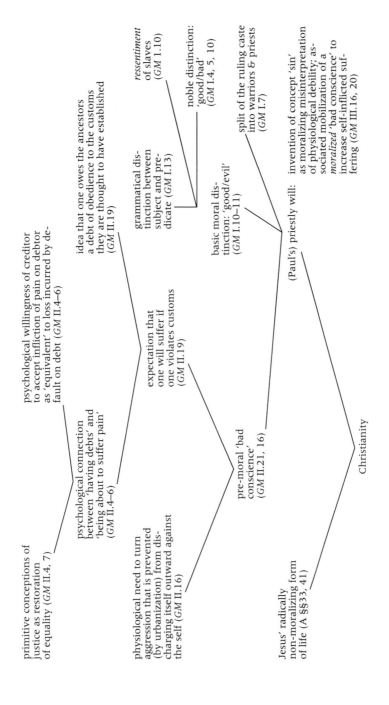

primitive conceptions of justice as restoration of equality (*GM* II.4, 7)

psychological willingness of creditor to accept infliction of pain on debtor as 'equivalent' to loss incurred by default on debt (*GM* II.4–6)

idea that one owes the ancestors a debt of obedience to the customs they are thought to have established (*GM* II.19)

grammatical distinction between subject and predicate (*GM* I.13)

*ressentiment* of slaves (*GM* I.10)

noble distinction: 'good/bad' (*GM* I.4, 5, 10)

split of the ruling caste into warriors & priests (*GM* I.7)

basic moral distinction: 'good/evil' (*GM* I.10–11)

invention of concept 'sin' as moralizing misinterpretation of physiological debility; associated mobilization of a *moralized* 'bad conscience' to increase self-inflicted suffering (*GM* III.16, 20)

psychological connection between 'having debts' and 'being about to suffer pain' (*GM* II.4–6)

expectation that one will suffer if one violates customs (*GM* II.19)

(Paul's) priestly will:

physiological need to turn aggression that is prevented (by urbanization) from discharging itself outward against the self (*GM* II.16)

pre-moral 'bad conscience' (*GM* II.21, 16)

Christianity

Jesus' radically non-moralizing form of life (A §§33, 41)

having thus recognized the difference between Jesus and Paul, we could now strip away the Pauline 'interpretation' and we would get back to something that was *not* thus bi-partite, not an interpretation of something, but the way of life itself, a final stopping point, an absolute origin. That one can get back to the thing itself, unvarnished and uninterpreted, is an illusion. Unless one believes in miracles, Jesus' 'practice' itself has historical antecedents which could be genealogically analyzed.[24] In addition Jesus' way of life, although it is not constituted by explicit belief in a set of propositions of the kind Paul asserts, can be itself seen as a kind of 'interpretation'. For Nietzsche, I am 'interpreting' a situation by reacting to it in a certain way. If I recoil from it, I am interpreting it as repulsive; if I draw near to it, I am taking it to be attractive; if I pass by without reacting at all, I am treating the situation as irrelevant or insignificant. This, presumably, is one of the things Nietzsche means when he claims that life itself is a process of evaluating and giving preference (*JGB* §9). So Jesus' form of life itself, although not characterized by explicit theological beliefs of the Pauline kind, will have the same two-part structure: It will ultimately show itself as arising from an episode in which a certain will with a certain interpretation of things tries to take over a preexisting form of living and acting (although the 'interpretation' now won't, as in the later Pauline case, be essentially a question of affirming and believing propositions, but of acting, feeling and perceiving in a certain way). I can't tell you what Nietzsche thinks this antecedently existing mode of living (which Jesus took over and reinterpreted) was, because he doesn't say, but in *GM* Nietzsche claims that Jesus' 'good news' of universal love was *not* the reverse of 'Jewish hatred' but grew out of it as its crowning moment (*GM* I.8). It would be a mistake, I think, to interpret this as meaning that Jesus' love was not *really* love, but rather ('really') hate. It would also be a mistake to identify this transformation of hate into universal love (in the person of Jesus) with what Nietzsche calls 'the slave revolt in morality'

(*GM* I.7), the transformation of a valuation based on the contrast 'good/bad' into a valuation based on a contrast between 'good' and 'evil'. Paul is a central figure in the slave revolt which lies in the main line of development of modern Western morality; Jesus, on the other hand, was, for Nietzsche, only very marginally associated with the genesis of 'our' morality. *Both* arise out of the deepest and most sublime hatred that ever was on earth, but each transforms this hatred in a completely different direction: Paul into a form of guilt-ridden, moralizing asceticism, and Jesus by becoming virtually a 'free spirit' *avant la lettre,* a man incapable of negating or refuting (*A* §32) with no conception of sin, guilt, or punishment (*A* §33). When Nietzsche sums up his campaign against traditional morality, the formula he uses is not 'Dionysos against Jesus' but: 'Dionysos against The Crucified' (last sentence of *EH*), 'The Crucified' being of course, the name of Paul's God (*First Corinthians* I, 18ff.)

IV

Alexander Nehamas is doubtless right to claim that for Nietzsche 'genealogy' is not some particular kind of method or special approach, rather it 'simply *is* history, correctly practiced'.[25] So 'Why do genealogy?', means 'Why do history?'. Nietzsche has a long early essay on the topic of the value of history which comes to the conclusion that history, like all forms of knowledge must be put at the service of 'life'; if thus subjected to the demands of 'life' history has genuine, if strictly limited, value. If, on the other hand, history escapes from the 'supervision and surveillance' of 'life' and establishes itself as a scientific discipline pursued for its own sake, it becomes a dangerous cancer which, if unchecked, can sap the vitality of the culture in which it arises.[26]

In the *Genealogy of Morality* Nietzsche says he is trying to answer two questions:

17

1. What is the value of (our) morality? (*GM* 'Preface' §§3, 5, 6)
2. What is the significance of ascetic ideals? (*GM* III.1, 2, 5 etc.)

The two questions are connected for Nietzsche because our morality is an ascetic one.

The answer to the first question is that at the moment (our) morality has overwhelmingly negative value as a major hindrance to the enhancement of life. The rest of the full answer to this question, though, is that in the past (and perhaps in some special circumstances in the present, too) traditional morality with its asceticism had the positive value of seducing inherently weak and despairing creatures who would otherwise have been tempted to do away with themselves into continuing to live, by giving their suffering (which actually resulted from their own weakness) an imaginary meaning. Any meaning, though, even a fantastic metaphysical meaning based on lies and gross misapprehensions, is better than none at all (*GM* III.13, 20, 28). Thus ascetic morality in the past has been a useful morality for the weak, one that allowed the maximal life-enhancement possible for *them* (given their naturally limited possibilities); it was a trick life itself used to outwit the weak and preserve itself under difficult circumstances when drastic measures were the only ones that would work.[27]

To understand the second question ('What is the significance of ascetic ideals?') and Nietzsche's answer to it, one must first recall his doctrine of 'significance' (*GM* II.12–13). Things don't *'have'* significance or meaning; they are *given* it. So the question 'What is the significance of ascetic ideals?' is incomplete; the full version would have to read: 'What is the significance of ascetic ideals for. . . . ?' where the blank is filled in by some specification of a particular group of people or what I earlier called an 'agency'. In the third part of *The Genealogy of Morals* Nietzsche explicitly discusses this question, filling in the blank in two different ways. First: 'What is the significance of ascetic ideals for artists, philosophers, and others engaged in various creative endeavours?' The answer is that a certain asceticism is part of the natural conditions under which certain forms of creativity flourish – if one wants to paint well, one can't quite be drunk *all* the time, so some minimal forms of self-restraint can be expected to be willed by painters as preconditions of their creativity; that then will be the significance of such ideals for them (*GM* III.1–9). The second form of the question is: 'What is the significance of ascetic ideals for religiously serious Christians?' The answer to this is that for Christians ascetic ideals have value in themselves – they aren't just seen as valuable because they are the natural conditions under which something *else* (for instance, creativity) will flourish. To be more exact the Christian wills ascetic ideals in order to undermine life, vitality, and the will itself; the (Christian) ascetic is a 'self-contradiction' (*GM* III.13).

There is, of course, a third way to ask the question, namely 'What is the significance of ascetic ideals for Nietzsche?' That is, given Nietzsche's account of the 'meaning' of significance, how does *he* propose to get mastery of these ascetic ideals and impose upon them his own *new* function and meaning?

In one of his unpublished notes (*WM* §915) Nietzsche writes that he wishes to 'renaturalize asceticism' with the goal of strengthening not negating the will. 'Strengthening the will' and 'enhancing life' seem to be more or less the same thing here, so it seems that Nietzsche's intention is to take over the traditional way of life associated with the ascetic ideal and renaturalize its asceticism in the interests of the enhancement and affirmation of life. In this context it is perhaps relevant to recall that for Nietzsche science and the will-to-truth itself are instances of the 'ascetic ideal' (*GM* III.23–27, *FW* §344). Up to now, Nietzsche thinks, the acquisition of scientific truth has been seen as intrinsically and absolutely valuable, but this demand that we *know* as much of the truth as possible derives from a prior demand that we always *tell* the truth, never deceive others or ourselves, and this is a moral demand. It is presumably an instance of the 'ascetic ideal' because it requires that we tell the truth even when that is contrary to what we would want and what would be good for us (*GM* I.1). So Nietzsche's programme of renaturalizing asceticism for the sake of enhancing life would mean, for instance, in the case of science and the pursuit of truth taking over the various habits, modes of thinking and acting, institutions, etc. associated with science and truth-telling, detaching them from the idea that they represent any value in themselves or have any absolute standing, and transforming them in such a way that they are turned into natural conditions for the enhancement of life (and are seen to be such). The way asceticism was made to contribute concretely to the enhancement of life would then be its 'significance'.

It still isn't clear what role genealogy (or, history) can play in this process. The purpose and effect of a genealogy can't be to criticize values or valuations directly. Nietzsche asserts very clearly that nothing about the history of the emergence or development of a set of valuations could have direct bearing on its value (*FW* §345, *WM* §254) – neither can history 'support' or 'legitimize' such value-claims (as tracing a pedigree presupposes), nor can any historical account in any way undermine a form of valuation. A form of valuation has the value it has – that is, for Nietzsche, it makes the contribution it can make to enhancing or negating life – and its origin or history is a separate issue. To be sure, a genealogy *can* undermine various *beliefs* about the origins of different forms of valuation. If I have a certain form of valuation I may need to believe certain things – if I am a Christian I may need to believe certain things about the origin of Christian forms of valuation. So if those beliefs are undermined, I may feel my values undermined, too, but this is as it were *my* problem, not part of the intention of the genealogy. For Nietzsche as genealogist: '. . . the value of a prescrip-

20

tion "Thou shalt" . . . is completely independent of . . . the opinions [people might have] about it and from the weeds of error with which it was perhaps overgrown . . .' just as the value of a medicine is independent of what the sick person *thinks* about it (*FW* §345).

It is a particular and idiosyncratic problem of Christianity that it cultivates truthfulness and introspection and is a form of valuation which requires its devotees to make claims and have beliefs that won't stand up to truthful introspective scrutiny (such as that moral action arises from altruistic sources). This means that Christianity dissolves itself (*GM* III.27; *FW* §357) and Nietzsche's genealogy will contribute to that process. That genealogy is experienced by the Christian as a form of criticism need not imply that that is how it looks from the perspective of genealogists themselves. For the Christian it may be a terrible indictment of Christianity that it requires its devotees to lie to themselves (and others). For Nietzsche it is a fact that Christianity is a tissue of lies, but this fact is of no particular evaluative significance; he has no objection to lying *per se*, but only to those forms of lying that in fact sap human vitality, turn the will against itself, denigrate life, or stunt 'the growth of the plant "man"' (*JGB* §44; cf. *EH* 'Why I am a Destiny' §7).

A genealogy of Christianity/modern morality/ascetics ideals won't *in itself* legitimize or justify Nietzsche's new positive valuation of life/will, and isn't in itself a criticism of alternative valuations. What a new form of valuation does, it will be recalled, is take over and reinterpret existing forms of living and acting. 'Science' in Nietzsche's wide sense of that term (which includes philology and history) is one part of our existing form of life. It has a value which is independent of its origin in the Christian ascetic ideal (because value is independent of origin, *FW* §345). The same is true specifically of the 'grey' science of history/genealogy (*GM* 'Preface' §7), a science which makes extensive use of our 'sense for *facts,* the last and most valuable of our senses' (*A* §59) to discover 'what is documented, what

21

can really be ascertained, what was really there' (*GM* 'Preface' §7). Nietzsche's genealogy then can start from his own 'historical and philological training' (*GM* 'Preface' §3) and has at its disposal a rich pre-existing set of sensibilities, ways of proceeding, canons of evidence, notions of what is more plausible and what less plausible (*GM* 'Preface' §4).

Nietzsche clearly thinks he can give an historically more accurate and plausible account of the emergence and development of our Christian morality from the perspective of his own new positive valuation of life than Christians themselves can from the standpoint of their own ascetic ideals. Christian truthfulness (and the apparatus of scientific history it gives rise to) will do in the Christian account of the development of our morality, leaving the field to Nietzsche's account. If Nietzsche's account is in this sense 'better' he will, he thinks, have succeeded in 'taking over' or 'gaining mastery of' a significant part of our existing form of life.

Nietzsche's genealogy of our ascetic morality doesn't yield a direct 'justification' of his positive valuation of the will and life, but the fact that he can from his perspective give a genealogy that is *more* acceptable to the grey science (on that science's own terms) than traditional accounts are, might be thought to provide a kind of indirect justification of Nietzsche's valuation. Whether or not this is the best way to think about this issue depends very much on what exactly one means by 'justification'.

Nietzsche's ability to give a genealogy of Christian morality which is historically superior to any other available certainly doesn't show that his positive valuation of life is 'true': 'Judgments, value-judgments about life, pro or contra, can in the final analysis never be true; they have value only as symptoms. . . .' (*GD* 'The Problem of Socrates' §2). There are, Nietzsche thinks, no non-circular, non-contextual standards with reference to which such a value-judgment about life itself could vindicate itself. In the final analysis there is just self-affirmation (of life) or the reverse.

Nietzsche also clearly does not believe that it in any way follows from this that our whole fabric of factual discourse is simply abolished, annulled, or reduced to some kind of arbitrary play of volitions. History in the service of life can and must be *better* history than history purportedly pursued for its own sake, for the sake of the 'truth', or as an end in itself.

For Nietzsche the success of his genealogy, the fact that it is better history than alternatives, is a sign or symptom of the greater vitality of the perspective from which the genealogy was carried out. This is of great importance to Nietzsche because he judges things by the vitality they exhibit, and that the perspective which gives the highest value to life-enhancement shows itself to possess the highest vitality is for Nietzsche no tautology or triviality. It might in principle have been that a perspective devoted to the pursuit of pure science for its own sake had the greatest vitality (i.e. produced the greatest number of particular interesting hypotheses that turned out to be plausible and well-supported by the evidence, gave fruitful guidance for the organization of social life, contributed to the flourishing of the arts, etc.).

For those of us not able to adopt Nietzsche's perspective and form of valuation it would perhaps be sufficient that his genealogy gives a more plausible and well-supported account of our puzzling history than other available alternatives (if that turned out to be the case).[28]

REFERENCES

Deleuze, G. (1962), *Nietzsche et la philosophie*. Paris: Presses Universitaires de France.

Foucault, M. (1971), 'Nietzsche, la généalogie, l'histoire', in *Hommage à Jean Hyppolite*. Paris: Presses Universitaires de France.

Foucault, M. (1983), 'On the Genealogy of Ethics: An Overview of
Work in Progress', in H. Dreyfus and P. Rabinow, *Michel Foucault:
Beyond Structuralism and Hermeneutics*. Chicago: The University of
Chicago Press.

Habermas, J. (1970), *Erkenntnis und Interesse*. Frankfurt a. M.:
Suhrkamp.

Habermas, J. (1983), 'Die Verschlingung von Mythos und
Aufklärung', in K.-H. Bohrer (ed.) *Mythos und Moderne*. Frankfurt
a.M.: Suhrkamp.

Homer (1951), *The Iliad*, translated by Richmond Lattimore. Chicago:
The University of Chicago Press.

Nehamas, A. (1985), *Nietzsche: Life as Literature*. Cambridge, Massachu-
setts: Harvard University Press.

Nietzsche, F. (1874), *Unzeitgemässe Betrachtungen. Zweites Stück: Vom
Nutzen und Nachteil der Historie für das Leben*, in Nietzsche (1980).
English translation: 'On the Use and Abuse of History', in *Untimely
Meditations*, trans. Hollingdale. Cambridge: Cambridge University
Press, 1983.

Nietzsche, F. (1901), *Der Wille zur Macht: Versuch einer Unwertung aller
Werte*, ausgewählt und geordnet von Peter Gast unter Mitwirkung
von Elisabeth Förster-Nietzsche. Stuttgart: Kröner.

Nietzsche, F. (1980), *Sämtliche Werke: Kritische Studienausgabe in 15
Bänden*, edited by G. Colli and M. Montinari. Berlin: Walter de
Gruyter.

Rorty, R. (1982), *The Consequences of Pragmatism*. Minneapolis: The
University of Minnesota Press.

*The following abbreviations are used in the text for works by Nietzsche:*

A   = *The Anti-Christ*
EH  = *Ecce Homo*
FW  = *The Gay Science*
GD  = *The Twighlight of the Idols*
GM  = *The Genealogy of Morality*
GT  = *The Birth of Tragedy*
JGB = *Beyond Good and Evil*
M   = *Daybreak*
WM = *The Will to Power*

These works are cited according to the Colli-Montinari edition of the
collected works (Nietzsche 1980), with the exception of *WM* which is
cited according to the sections of the old Gast edition (Nietzsche 1901).

English translations by Walter Kaufmann are widely available in paperback. (The new translation of *Genealogy,* ed. K. Ansell-Pearson (Cambridge University Press, 1994) is superior to the Kaufmann translation.)

NOTES

1 Foucault (1971).
2 Foucault (1984).
3 Homer (1951), Book II, lines 100 ff.
4 Note that Lattimore translates the same Greek word ('skêptron') sometimes as 'sceptre' but often as 'staff' (e.g. Homer (1951) Book I, line 14; Book I, line 28; Book II, line 199).
5 The treatment of Thersites in the *Iliad* is a good instance of what Nietzsche claims was a central characteristic of an aristocratic society. Thersites' criticisms of Agamemnon are virtually the same as those voiced by Achilleus (cf. Homer (1951), Book II, lines 225 ff. with Homer (1951), Book I, lines 149 ff.), but whereas the Greeks (including Agamemnon) are quickly wooing Achilleus with gifts and apologies, Thersites is only beaten and laughed at (Homer (1951), Book II, lines 265–77). This does seem to be a society in which the content of what is said is less important than who it is who says it.
6 In Book I Achilleus has already given a very different account of the sceptre he holds while speaking in the assembly. (Unfortunately it isn't clear whether or not this is the same one Hephaistos gave Zeus, who gave Argeiphontes . . .)

> By this sceptre which never again will bear leaf nor
> branch, now that it has left behind the cut stump in the mountains,
> nor shall it ever blossom again, since the bronze blade stripped
> bark and leafage, and now at last the sons of the Achaians
> carry it in their hand in state when they administer
> the justice of Zeus.
>
> (Homer (1951), Book I, lines 224 ff.)

To say that Hephaistos 'wrought' the sceptre for Zeus presumably means that he made and inserted the gold studs or nails with which the wooden body of the sceptre was adorned – after all, Hephaistos was essentially a smith (Homer (1951), Book XVIII, lines 368 ff.) not a carpenter. So Hephaistos' making of the sceptre for Zeus is perhaps not the natural origin or stopping point it may seem to be. The wood for the body of a sceptre must have come from somewhere, so perhaps there is a step in the succession before the fitting of the golden studs. The administration of the justice of Zeus requires someone to go out into the mountains to cut down an appropriate branch and strip off the bark and leafage. Cutting things down with the bronze blade, however, is just what Achilleus is good at.

7 For a key to abbreviations used in referring to Nietzsche's works, see References.

8 In tracing a pedigree one is positioned, as it were, at the singular point of 'origin' and invited to look 'down' the chain of succession (from Hephaistos to Agamemnon), whereas in a genealogy one stands with Ego and looks back 'up' the lines of transmission at the seemingly unlimited and ramifying series of ancestors.

9 At *M* §44 Nietzsche asserts that the closer we get to the 'origin' (*Ursprung*) of things, the less possible it is for us to evaluate what we find; our forms of evaluation simply become increasingly irrelevant. The realm of origins is the realm of radical insignificance, not of heightened meaningfulness. Oddly enough, Habermas (1970, p. 356) cites and discusses this very passage, but seems not to have recognized its implications.

10 Cf. *JGB* §257.

11 One might wonder whether *M* §44 (our forms of valuation can get less and less purchase the further back toward the 'origins' we move) is compatible with *GM* II.6 (the beginnings of everything great are doused in blood). This difficulty disappears if one keeps in mind that for Nietzsche there are no absolute 'origins' or 'beginnings'; an 'origin' is a relative stopping point picked out for one or another reason, but 'behind' which there will stand a history (which one could investigate if one had some reason to do so). It is perfectly coherent to think that the period of the recent past (from three thousand to, say, five hundred years ago) was an especially nasty patch and one of particular importance for understanding how various contemporary phenomena have come to be the way they are, but also that the further back one goes the more difficult it becomes to apply our forms of valuation.

12 Jürgen Habermas (1983), p. 425.

13 Cf. *FW* §377; *JGB* §30, §40, §202f, §242, §44; *A* §57.

14 Jürgen Habermas (1983), pp. 421ff.

15 The passage actually reads:

> . . . Whence might science then have taken its unconditional belief, its conviction, on which it rests, that truth is more important than any

other thing, even than any other conviction. Precisely this conviction [i.e. that truth is more important than anything else, R. G.] could not have arisen if truth *and* untruth both had shown themselves continuously as useful, as is the case.

16 Nietzsche was clearly fascinated by this Romantic view that the truth about human life is literally unbearable to most humans – one finds it already in *GT* §3. One of the traditional functions of art for Nietzsche is to produce 'worlds of appearance' (*Schein*) which will hide the horrid truth from us and allow us to survive (cf. *GT* §7). The 'ascetic priest' in the third essay of *GM* is not only a physician and shepherd (III.15) but also an 'artist' in feelings of guilt (III.15): By creating an illusory 'sense' for human suffering ('You are suffering *because* you are guilty'; cf. III.15–20) the priest seduces humans into continuing to live (III.13).

17 Cf. also *JGB* §1.

18 There is another version of 'pragmatism' to be found, for example in the works of Richard Rorty (cf. Rorty (1982)) which seeks not to 'define' but dispense with a philosophical definition of truth. I adopt the view in the main text because I believe it closer to what those who attribute to Nietzsche a 'pragmatist' conception of truth (e.g. Habermas) would mean by 'pragmatism'.

19 Habermas (1983), p. 422.

20 Habermas (1983), p. 424.

21 Nietzsche seems to use 'meaning' (*Bedeutung*) and 'sense' (*Sinn*) more or less interchangeably, at least in the contexts that are relevant for the discussion of 'genealogy' and so I won't try to distinguish them.

22 Obviously I see no reductionist implications in the claim that a certain event, such as, for example, the Protestant Reformation can be seen as at the same time an attempt to get mastery of Christian life and an attempt to reinterpret it.

23 Nietzsche's view is incompatible with any 'dialectical' conception of history (at least one in the tradition of Hegel). A process can be described as 'dialectical' if it unfolds endogenously according to an inherent logic. For Nietzsche the 'wills' that come to struggle over a form of life characteristically come from *outside* that form and their encounter is contingent in that no outcome of it is more inherently 'logical' than any other. On Nietzsche as anti-dialectician, cf. G. Deleuze (1962).

24 Although I must admit that there is one passage (*A* §32) that might conceivably be read as incompatible with the view I present here.

Nietzsche says that Jesus' 'good news' is not something he had to acquire by struggle: 'it is there, it is from the beginning . . .'

25 Nehamas (1985), p. 246, footnote 1.

26 Nietzsche (1874).

27 The attribution of what seems to be some kind of metaphysical agency to 'life' in passages like *GM* III.13 and *GD* 'Morality as Counter-Nature' §5 seems to me one of Nietzsche's least inspired and most unfortunate ideas.

28 I have profited from helpful comments on a draft of this essay by Michael Hardimon (MIT), Michael Rosen (Lincoln College, Oxford), and Quentin Skinner (Christ's College, Cambridge).

# 2

## KULTUR, BILDUNG, GEIST

THE attempt to say anything both general and useful about the concept of 'culture' might seem doomed from the very start.[1] In their well-known discussion Kroeber and Kluckhohn distinguish literally dozens of different senses in which the word 'culture' is used.[2] One might think that if the anti-essentialist line deriving from Nietzsche and the late Wittgenstein which is now dominant in the humanities has any plausibility at all, then surely here.[3] If there is no single feature all games have in common by reference to which they are all called 'games' then *a fortiori* it seems unlikely that anything much of interest could be said about the nature of 'culture' in general. If it is further the case that different languages cut up the world differently, it might be thought merely to compound the difficulties of an already hopeless situation to discuss purported analogues to the English term 'culture' in another language. That, however, is what I propose to do for reasons I will now try to explain.

Human beings who have had some experience of our world have repeatedly made two kinds of observations about it. The first is that members of any given human group often behave in ways that are very much alike, yet differ systematically from the ways in which members of other groups behave (in similar circumstances). As Herodotus points out, Greeks cremate their dead fathers and would be horrified at the proposal that they should eat them, whereas Indians ('of the tribe called Callatiae') eat their dead parents and would be shocked by the suggestion that they should burn them.[4] Children are generally brought up to conform with the habits of the group to which they (or their parents) belong. We speak here of different traditional practices, folkways, customs, and so on. The second kind of observation humans make is that some people are better at engaging in certain valued forms of activity than others: some can run faster than others, control themselves more fully under conditions of stress, speak more convincingly, hit a moving animal with a missile more often, paint more beautiful pictures, and so on. At least for the past two thousand years or so people in Europe have noticed that for at least some of these forms of activity performance can be improved by cultivating existing aptitudes. People begin to train for races, exercise themselves in forms of self-control, and so on.

In practice, of course, folkways and forms of valuation are inextricably intertwined; one of the things that will be customary in a society will be to value certain things in a certain way and to cultivate certain forms of achievement. Herodotus's Greeks and Indians didn't just differ in their habits for disposing of dead relatives, but each group thought its own way *better.* Herodotus even claims that it is a general truth that people on reflection will always prefer their own customs. Customary forms of differential valuation will themselves be infinitely varied. In some cases relatively clear and determinate criteria will be available – some people can run consistently faster than others and it isn't hard to agree on who runs fastest – but in other cases even the crudest kind of comparison will be difficult and controversial – who is the best painter? what particular form of self-restraint in what circumstances is better than what forms of flamboyance? Thinking about 'culture' has been a series of attempts to put together coherently experience of the variability of human folkways with people's sense that some ways of doing things and behaving are better than others and deserve to be cultivated. Given the obscurity, indeterminateness, and complexity of this task it isn't very surprising that the history of our thinking about these issues has been tangled and inchoate.

For a number of very good reasons we are suspicious nowadays of claims that one culture is superior to others, whether that means that the folkways of one group are overall better than those of another or that high culture is to be privileged over popular entertainment. Still, there is something self-deluded and hypocritical about some of the more extreme forms this suspicion has taken. As Nietzsche pointed out, *'Leben ist Abschätzen'*[5] and it isn't realistic to pretend we could go through life without choosing, preferring one thing to another, influencing those we come in contact with in one direction or another, cultivating certain of our abilities at the expense of others, and so on. It isn't altogether clear, though, what room there is between the suspicion and the realism.

Perhaps one can make some progress here by considering a concrete historical example of ways in which people have thought about 'culture'. I propose to see if we can find some enlightenment by looking at a body of theorizing that is not very far removed from us in space and time, but which contrasts sharply with some of the assumptions we are inclined to make, a tradition of theorizing which is consciously and explicitly based on the assumption that some forms of culture are superior and others inferior. The example is the way the sphere of 'culture' was understood in Germany in the late eighteenth, the nineteenth, and the early twentieth centuries.

I

In German there are three words that are used in place of our 'culture': *Kultur, Bildung,* and *Geist.* The first two of these terms have 'shadows', that is, terms that are semantically closely related to the original ones, but which gradually become more and more sharply distinguished from the original term until finally a contrasting pair arises. In the case of *Kultur* the shadow is *Zivilisation*. *Kultur* and *Zivilisation* start at no great distance from one another and even have a range of more or less overlapping usage, but by the beginning of the twentieth century the two terms have begun to be used as members of a contrasting pair: *Zivilisation* has a mildly pejorative connotation and was used to refer to the external trappings, artifacts, and amenities of an industrially highly advanced society and also to the overly formalistic and calculating habits and attitudes that were thought to be characteristic of such societies. In some highly developed versions two forms of *Zivilisation* could be distinguished, one (the 'French' form) concerned with the virtues of a courtly society – concern for appearance, indirectness, diplomacy – the other (the 'British' form) with the virtues of commercial society – calculation, egoism, sobriety.

*Kultur* was then used to refer to positively valorized habits, attitudes, and properties. During the period immediately before and during World War I the contrast became a staple of German journalism: The French and British have *Zivilisation*, Germans have *Kultur*.[6] German honesty and directness are contrasted with French insincerity on the one hand, and British calculation on the other. In the strongest versions of this view *Kultur* and *Zivilisation*[7] are actually considered *opposites*.[8]

*Bildung* has as its shadow *Erziehung*. Both *Bildung* and *Erziehung* (and their associated linguistic forms) refer to processes of training, education, or formation. One linguistic difference between the two terms is that while *Erziehung* is used only to refer to the process of education or training, *Bildung* can be used to refer either to a process of formation or to the form imparted in such a process. A further difference is that *Erziehung* is generally used of a process that one person or group inflicts on another; thus a parent would be said to train a child to conform to certain social expectations and observers would speak of the child's *Erziehung*. *Bilden*, the verb from which *Bildung* is derived, can also be used in cases in which one person imposes a form on another, but increasingly *Bildung* as a noun comes to be used for processes of *self*-cultivation (and their results).[9]

In what follows I would like first to say something about Kant's views on the general phenomenon of 'culture'. These represent a kind of common European-Enlightenment baseline against which I will try to delineate three lines of conceptual development which dominate thinking about culture in Germany during the nineteenth and early twentieth centuries.

II

In his *Critique of Judgment* (1790) Kant distinguished between what he calls *Kultur* and what he calls *Zivilisierung*. *Kultur*, he claims, is the process of rendering a rational creature serviceable 'for any purposes whatever' (or the result of such a process when it has been successful).[10] A rational creature is, according to Kant, serviceable for various purposes to the extent to which it satisfies two conditions: a) it has acquired skills, and b) it has "discipline" (*Disziplin* or *Zucht*)[11] which for Kant means that the rational creature in question has a will capable of resisting the despotism of desire (§83). This notion of *Kultur* is completely asocial: Robinson Crusoe on his island could discipline his will as firmly as a person who lived in a large nineteenth-century city; indeed, he might be more likely to acquire a large and varied body of skills than a city-dweller, if only because he would be more highly motivated to do so. *Kultur* as general cultivation of one's faculties is at least in principle equally accessible to all rational agents regardless of their particular social circumstances. *Zivilisierung*, on the other hand, is for Kant a specifically social property (§41). I am *zivilisiert* to the extent to which I have the inclination and skill to communicate to others the pleasure I take in certain objects; a *zivilisiert* person wishes to have pleasure in an object which can be shared with a community of others. *Kultur* and *Zivilisierung* seem thus to be distinct, but they are by no means mutually exclusive, much less opposed the one to the other. I might well both have skills and a disciplined will, and incline to those forms of pleasure I can enjoy sharing with others. For that matter, given that skill in communicating my pleasure also increases my serviceability as a rational creature, the cultivation of rhetorical or literary talent might make me both more cultured and more civilized.[12]

### III

The first of the three strands of development away from this position which I wish to discuss gets started when Herder begins to claim that there is a plurality of different, nationally specific ways of living, each with its own particular way of viewing the world, its own characteristic virtues and achievements, its own desires, ambitions, and ideals, and each in principle of equal value. Herder very much stresses the internal coherence of each of these ways of life. Such a way of living is not just a random collection of traits, but rather a unified whole of parts that 'fit together'. He doesn't have a single term (such as *Kultur* or *Geist*) which he invariably uses to designate these plural distinctive ways of living, experiencing, and valuing. He doesn't in general share Kant's penchant for creating a distinctive technical vocabulary. His view of the multiplicity of human ways of living is, as it were, mirrored in his flexible linguistic usage: he speaks of different 'forms of thinking' (*Denkart*), different forms of customary morality (*Sitten*), different forms of education (both *Erziehung* and *Bildung*), different 'national characters' (*Nationalcharaktere*),[13] and even of different forms of 'national happiness' (*Nationalglückseligkeit*) arising from the satisfaction of different 'national inclinations' (*National-neigungen*).[14] Despite this pluralism about national ways of life, Herder's use of the term *Kultur* is still that of Kant and the Enlightenment: it refers to the general state or level of cultivation of human faculties. As has been pointed out, Herder never uses the word *Kultur* in the plural.[15]

In the early nineteenth century this Herderian conception of a plurality of nations, peoples, and folkways gets taken up, but usually without Herder's assumption that each nation has its centre of gravity in itself and its own value, and also generally still without the use of the term *Kultur* to designate in a theoretically emphatic way what it is that makes for the difference between nations or peoples.[16]

One of the most important political issues in central Europe at the beginning of the nineteenth century is what attitude to take toward the ideals of the French Revolution and toward the fact of Napoleon. Pluralist arguments like those one finds in Herder come to be deployed as forms of resistance to the French[17]: local German legal codes are not inferior to the Code Napoléon, although by Enlightenment standards they may seem less 'rational'; after all, the legal code of a society should be suited to the historically rooted characteristic attitudes, inclinations, beliefs, and customs of the population and these are different in France and in the various parts of territory inhabited by speakers of German.[18]

Eventually the claims that German institutions and ways of doing things are as good as French, just different, get turned into claims of national superiority. One important step in this long process is the series of lectures the philosopher Fichte gave in French-occupied Berlin in 1807, the *Reden an die deutsche Nation*. Given the political situation Fichte had to express himself with some circumspection, but the basic point is unmistakable: the German 'nation' is superior to the French on the grounds of its greater 'primordiality' (*Ursprünglichkeit*) and this 'primordiality' is a more or less fixed trait of the national character which finds its various expressions in customs, ways of feeling and thinking, attitudes, and so on.[19]

The terms in which he couches his reaction to things French are not original to Fichte. In the 1760s Lessing (in his *Hamburgische Dramaturgie*) had contrasted the contrived, artificial, shallow plays of Voltaire with the more realistic, spontaneous, directly forceful works of Shakespeare.[20] His intention in doing this had been to put an end to the monopoly French plays and (bad) imitations of French plays exercised over the German stage at the time and to propose Shakespeare as a more appropriate model for a future German theatre. It seems unlikely that it would have occurred to someone like Lessing that this could be taken as implying a general superiority of the German (or English) nation over the French. Claims about the superior rude vigor of the Germanic peoples go back, of course, at least to Tacitus (*Germania*).[21]

The basic properties of a people which are 'primordial' for Fichte are vitality, sincerity, lack of egotism (*Selbstsucht*), diligence, and independence (*Selbständigkeit*).[22] One should not make the mistake of thinking that because the attitudes, habits, and beliefs that are authentically German are 'primordial' they will arise and maintain themselves spontaneously, at least under modern circumstances. Fichte proposes in the *Reden* a comprehensive system of 'national education' (*Nationalerziehung*) which was not to be restricted to the old 'educated classes' but to encompass all members of the *Volk* and which would inculcate in them the correct 'primordial' German attitudes.[23] Fichte develops this nationalist programme without actually using the term *Kultur* at all. Rather he speaks of various forms of 'education' (*Bildung* and *Erziehung*, and especially the above-mentioned *Nationalerziehung*).[24]

In retrospect it is the relative absence of the term *Kultur* in the period from 1800 to 1870 that is most striking.[25] I strongly suspect that this absence is not unrelated to the pervasive influence of Hegel and his followers in the 1820s, 1830s, and 1840s. Hegelianism tended to prevent the term *Kultur* from establishing itself because Hegel's notion of *Geist* preempted the conceptual space in which uses of *Kultur* could take root.[26] Hegelianism acknowledges the superficial plurality of historically specific folkways, forms of art, sociability, religion, and so on, but sees them all as having an underlying unity, as being mere forms of a historically developing structure, *Geist,* whose internal structure Hegel's philosophy articulates. In such a scheme there is no place for a separate concept of *Kultur.*

Only in the 1870s, when Hegel's star had long since set, does the term *Kultur* begin to be used to refer to a plurality of nationally distinct ways of living, thinking, and valuing. In *Menschliches, Allzumenschliches* (1878) Nietzsche discusses various different national 'cultures' in the context of trying to find some principle for rank-ordering them, and in fact in the first of the *Unzeitgemässe Betrachtungen* (1873) he had felt obliged to argue against the view that the outcome of the Franco-Prussian War represented a victory of 'German culture' over 'French culture'.[27] By the time of the First World War this kind of usage had become common. That Max Weber in 1915 could blithely write 'All culture today is and remains bound to a nation' (*'ist und bleibt durchaus national gebunden'*)[28] indicates the distance that has been traveled from Kant's use of the term *Kultur.*[29]

IV

The first of the three strands of development was about 'culture' as a collective phenomenon (even if, as I claim, the word *Kultur* was not itself used). Now I would like to go on to a second line of development which I will associate with (Wilhelm von) Humboldt and Goethe and which centers around a notion of culture that is individual and progressive. The term most usually used for this notion is *Bildung.*

Humboldt in his famous essay on the limits of state action (1792) claims that the goal of humanity is the full development of the powers of each human individual. In itself (at least in this vague and unspecific form) this is not a terribly original claim. In his *Critique of Judgment* Kant had asserted that our 'natural end' (*Naturzweck*) is to develop our powers and capacities (§83). Kant calls this process of development (and its result) *Kultur.* Humboldt calls it *Bildung* and goes on to claim that since

37

each individual has a unique configuration of powers, if each person were able to participate in the fullest possible process of *Bildung* the result would be just so many different, highly individuated persons. Humboldt uses this as an argument for a positive valuation of the role of social diversity (and a limitation on the role of the state in providing for the welfare of its citizens). The more the circumstances which individuals encounter in their lives differ, the more those individuals will be motivated to develop their diverse powers and capacities. State action directed at providing for the welfare of its citizens will both prevent the individual citizens from being self-active and will tend to create uniformity of conditions; this will have a deleterious effect on the *Bildung* of the individuals in the state.

At about the same time that Humboldt was writing his essay on the limits of state action Goethe was at work on a novel that would initiate a new sub-genre in German literature. The novel was *Wilhelm Meister* (1796) and the sub-genre was that of the *Bildungsroman*. *Wilhelm Meister* isn't just about the hero's cultivation and development of his powers and capacities, but is at least as much about his attempts to orient himself realistically in the world, to discover what is in fact possible and what he wishes to do with his life. Of these three elements – development of one's powers, discovery of one's true wants, and realistic acceptance of the world as it is – the early Romantics eagerly embraced the first two, but exhibited greater or less skepticism about the third. After an initial period of enthusiasm for Goethe's novel Novalis undertook to write a kind of anti-*Wilhelm Meister*, his unfinished novel *Heinrich von Ofterdingen*, which would show the hero progressing not from unrealistic adolescent dreams to an acceptance of the possibilities offered by the real world as it is, but rather as moving from conventional absorption in life as it is to a more 'poetic' form of existence.[30] Obviously one will get very different versions of the ideal of *Bildung* by emphasizing one or the other of the three components. In the political realm emphasis on self-development and self-discovery might be thought to point in the direction of some form of liberalism; emphasis on realistic adjustment to the world as it is might on the other hand be thought to have rather more politically quietist consequences.

## V

The third strand I want to mention is one which places aesthetic experience and judgment in the center of discussion. The main source of this in nineteenth-century Germany was the work of Friedrich Schiller (many of whose chief ideas, however, are just modifications of Kantian theses).[31] What I am calling the 'third strand' is itself an attempt to put together two things that don't *prima facie* seem to have much to do with each other.

The first of these two things is the view that aesthetic experience is the experience of a certain state of harmony between different parts of our mind or different components of our cognitive faculties. Roughly speaking this line of argument begins with the Kantian thought that more or less *any* kind of human experience requires the cooperative activity of various different human faculties; for Kant these include a certain faculty of direct apprehension, the imagination, and a faculty of conceptualization. The objects we encounter in the world can be of such a kind as to make this cooperation of our faculties difficult and laborious, or easy and fluent. An object is aesthetically pleasing if the play of our faculties which constitutes our experience of it is smooth, harmonious, and free. When we see a beautiful natural object it, as it were, effortlessly gives itself to us for apprehension; it is as if it had specifically been formed so as to make our apprehension of it easy. A work of art, of course (on this view), actually *has* been formed so as to make our apprehension of it fluent and free.

Schiller also accepts a basically Kantian view of ethics: an action has positive moral value if it accords with what reason demands and is performed by the agent *because* it is known to be what reason demands. However, Schiller argues, this Kantian analysis of morality, although correct as far as it goes, fails to address an issue that is in fact of great importance to us. For Kant the actual configuration of my empirical desires is not relevant to a determination of the moral quality of the action I perform. If reason requires me to do X, it makes no difference (at least to the moral evaluation of the act) whether I detest doing X and must force myself to do it (because it is what reason demands) or whether doing X accords with my own spontaneous inclination. Perhaps, Schiller admits, it makes no difference to the strictly ethical evaluation of an action whether I perform it with repugnance or zest (provided I perform it because it is what reason demands), but surely it does make a difference to what we consider to be the ideal form of human life and the ideal person. An ideal person leading a truly good life would be one who spontaneously wanted to do what reason demands, that is, whose actions were in unforced harmony with the demands of reason. Kant, to be sure, had had the thought of what he called a 'holy will', a will whose actions of themselves 'necessarily' conformed with the dictates of reason,[32] but the presence of the word 'necessarily' in his account of the holy will means that it couldn't be a realistic description of the will of an empirical human individual. When Schiller and others speak of an uncoerced harmony between inclination and the demands of reason, they don't mean a case in which the actions of the agent in question 'necessarily' conform to what is fully rational so that the agent couldn't possibly do anything other than what is in accordance with reason. Rather their idea is that through various processes of education and development a human might arrive at a state in which he or she 'could' (in whatever sense of 'could' is appropriate for human action) act against the demands of reason, but would have to act against their inclinations to act in a way that reason would not finally endorse.[33]

This is the point at which aesthetics reenters the discussion. Aesthetic education (*Erziehung*) can produce a kind of harmoniousness among my human faculties which predisposes me to do what reason requires easily, readily, and 'naturally', that is, without coercion by others or by myself.[34] Aesthetic experience and education can then be seen as a propaedeutic to morality. One of the most important tasks of 'culture' (*Kultur*) then is 'to make man aesthetic'.[35] Furthermore if I am in the appropriately harmonious state with spontaneous inclinations conformable to the demands of reason, then my moral action itself will have aesthetic properties. In performing my duty (that is, doing what reason requires) I will also be (and seem to be) spontaneously and naturally following my deepest inclinations; my action will then have the highly valued property Schiller calls 'grace' (*Anmut*).[36]

That is the first line of argument I wish to discuss under this third rubric. The second line of thought focuses not so much on aesthetic experience as on aesthetic judgment or judgments of taste. A specifically aesthetic judgment, it is claimed, is not like either a descriptive or an ethical judgment. Both descriptive and ethical judgments to some extent and perhaps in different ways *demand* my assent; a judgment of taste rather invites my agreement. It is essential to our notion of an aesthetic judgment, it is claimed, that we think that such a judgment can be communicated to others and thus shared with them, but that others' assent to it must be completely free and based on *their* own immediate experience. When claiming that something is 'beautiful' we are tacitly claiming that this judgment of ours would be the object of free, universal agreement. Art is a realm of shared, self-regulating subjectivity.[37]

The two lines of argument I have just described are sufficiently suggestive – each is sufficiently unspecific and their connection is sufficiently loose and unclear – to allow great scope for further interpretation and reinterpretation. In short, this is an ideal framework for an ideology; indeed until World War I

41

much of the popular theorizing about morality and art in Germany consisted in ringing changes upon the themes found in these two lines of argument.

The concrete sociopolitical embodiment of the idea of a self-regulating aesthetic society was the so-called *Bildungsbürgertum*, the 'educated middle classes', who, although excluded from the exercise of serious forms of independent political power virtually everywhere, used their purported possession of a cultivated faculty of aesthetic judgment, their taste, to legitimize the retention of a certain socially privileged position. Membership in this group, the *Bildungsbürgertum*, was not supposed to be guaranteed by noble birth, inherited wealth, or economic success, but was to be granted by the free recognition of one's (good) taste on the part of others who were themselves in a position to judge. The *Bildungsbürgertum* was a self-coopting group whose collective good taste was a tacit warrant (almost) of moral superiority.

VI

The creation of the Second Empire in 1871 transformed a plethora of small political units, many of them still ruled dynastically, into something that wished to present itself as the German nation-state (although it included large numbers of native speakers of Polish in the eastern bits of Prussia and excluded the German-speakers in the Habsburg lands and in Switzerland). The world of 'nation-states', however, had by the beginning of the twentieth century become a complex and highly competitive one and generated a perceived need for a set of terms to serve as vehicles for differential national self-congratulation. Full success could be attained only by finding a set of terms that could be used to assert superiority on both of two fronts, against the French in the west and the Slavic peoples in the east. Herder would be utterly useless in this context

42

because he lacked (or rather explicitly rejected) the notion that one nation could be superior to others in its form of life; *de facto* his work served to legitimize the incipient nationalisms of various Slavic peoples.[38] The concept of *Bildung* which had been so prominent in discussions between 1790 and 1870 also was not useful for marking the appropriate distinctions. Despite its use in compounds like *Bildungsbürgertum* the term *Bildung* never shed its strongly individualistic associations and wasn't ever completely taken over into the nationalist programme. Not even the most rabid nationalists could claim that *all* Germans were *gebildet* (in anything like the sense that term had come to have in normal parlance) and it would have been equally difficult plausibly to deny that at least some members of other national groups were *gebildet*.

Kant's distinction between *Kultur* and *Zivilisierung* (see above) would also not do the job. First of all Kant's distinction was not a sharp and exclusive one. Then also perhaps the French were more sociable and communicative and the Germans more skilled and disciplined, but that contrast was hardly one to make the heart beat quicker or send millions of men into the trenches. In addition since Kant was a conscious 'cosmopolitan' his position as a whole could have at best limited attraction for nationalists.

The solution that was found was essentially to take over the central part of Fichte's views about the greater 'primordiality' (spontaneity, sincerity, vigor, and so on) and greater self-discipline of the German nation (while silently passing over Fichte's emphasis on individual *Selbständigkeit*), and to express this view in terms Fichte himself did not use, as a superiority of German *Kultur*. The canonical way of making the nationalist contrast between Germany and the Entente at the time of the First World War, then, is in terms of a tripartite division between *Zivilisation* (France), *Kultur* (Germany), and *Barbarei* (Russia).[39]

VII

The conclusions I am able to draw from this excursion into conceptual history are meager and anodyne. We can't escape acting in preferential ways, valuation, and choice, and such valuation is complexly related to its social context. The nation-state might be as alive and well as it ever was,[40] but the idea that the final framework for valuation is and must be the nation-state seems merely quaint in the 1990s. Many of the preferences and valuations that give my life structure will be aesthetic, if by that is meant that they won't impinge in a sufficiently drastic and clear way on others for it to be reasonable to subject them to binding forms of organization. They won't, however, be 'aesthetic' in the very specific sense given that term in the Kantian tradition.

In some contexts it is important for the members of a group to become concerned about the coherency of their way of behaving and valuing or about their differentiation from other groups. However, important as such things sometimes are, it is also important not to make them occasions for excessive self-congratulation.

NOTES

1  This paper is a revised version of a talk I gave in January 1994 as part of a Round Table Discussion of the question 'What is Culture?' at King's College Research Centre in Cambridge. I'm grateful to the other members of the Round Table: Peter de Bolla, Ross Harrison, Stephen Hugh-Jones, and Chris Prendergast (all King's College) for help in beginning to think about this issue. Professors Michael Forster (University of Chicago), Pierre Keller (University of California/ Riverside), and Quentin Skinner (Christ's College) made very helpful comments on the original version of this paper. I have not been able to respond to all of their objections and comments adequately.
2  Alfred Kroeber and Clyde Kluckhohn, 'Culture: A Critical Review of Concepts and Definitions' in *Papers of the Peabody Museum of American Archeology and Ethnology* 47 (Cambridge, Mass., 1952).

3 Friedrich Nietzsche, *Zur Genealogie der Moral* (Leipzig, 1887), II. Abhandlung §§ 12, 13; Ludwig Wittgenstein, *Philosophische Untersuchungen* (Frankfurt am Main, 1952), §§ 1–240.

4 Herodotus, *Histories*, Book III, 38.

5 Nietzsche, *Jenseits von Gut und Böse* (Leipzig, 1885), § 9.

6 Cf. Jörg Fisch, 'Zivilisation, Kultur', in *Geschichtliche Grundbegriffe: Historisches Lexikon zur politisch-sozialen Sprache in Deutschland,* ed. Otto Brunner, Werner Conze, and Reinhardt Koselleck (Stuttgart, 1992), vol. 7.

7 In the case of two well-known books written in German the translator has seen fit to render *Kultur* as 'civilization', namely Jakob Burkhardt's *Kultur der Renaissance in Italien,* which becomes *The Civilization of the Renaissance in Italy,* and Freud's *Das Unbehagen in der Kultur,* which is known as *Civilization and its Discontents.* For reasons I can't go into here both of these works stand outside the main line of development I am trying to sketch here.

8 Thus Thomas Mann at the beginning of World War I (November, 1914) said: 'Civilisation (*Zivilisation*) and culture (*Kultur*) are not only not one and the same; they are opposites (*Gegensätze*)' ('*Gedanken im Kriege*', in *Die Neue Rundschau* [Bern, 1914], Band 2). Cf. also Nietzsche *WM* §121.

9 Cf. Rudolf Vierhaus, 'Bildung', in *Geschichtliche Grundbegriffe* (1972), vol. 1. Note that *Bildung* is not etymologically related to the English 'build'. *Bildung* comes from *Bild* (sign, image) and so means the process of imposing an image or form on something, or the results of such a process, whereas 'build' comes from a completely different Indo-European root having to do with 'dwelling'.

10 The Latin *cultura* of course just means taking care of or cultivating something (with the something often added in the genitive, as in *agri cultura, hortorum cultura,* and eventually *animi cultura*). This general sense of *cultura* was dominant for a long time.

11 The word *Zucht* would also repay study; it contains the same ambiguity as the English 'breeding', meaning both control of the mating behavior of animals (horse-breeding, dog-breeding, and so on) and having good manners. This ambiguity makes the term especially attractive to social Darwinists or those eager to extol the virtues of a hereditary aristocracy. For discussion of medieval books on good behavior at table (*Tischzucht*) cf. Norbert Elias, *Über den Prozess der Zivilisation* (Bern, 1969), I, 75ff. It is important not to be anachronistic in tracing what might seem to be early references to 'German culture'. Thus when the thirteenth-century poet Walter von

der Vogelweide in his poem 'Ir sult sprechen willekommen' describes his experiences of various countries and their differing customs (*site*) and declares that '*tiutschiu zuht gât vor in allen*' (which I take it means: 'In all the countries I have visited German breeding is preeminent') this is presumably not a reference to a nationally specific form of German culture, rather just a claim that Germans are in general more 'well-bred' by the commonly accepted Western European standards of such things. This may be a false or a self-serving claim but it is a completely different kind of claim from those one would find around the time of the First World War to the effect that there was a specifically German form of culture which was at the same time unique and superior to other forms of feeling, acting, and valuing. Walter, like everyone else, noticed differences in customs between different countries – how could one fail to notice that? – and also noticed differences in (level of) 'breeding' in different places. What he does *not* do, and what no one does until the end of the nineteenth century, is connect these two observations in the systematic way that later came to seem obvious, namely by reference to varying national cultures.

12 In his brief '*Idee zu einer allgemeinen Geschichte in weltbürgerlicher Absicht*' (1784) Kant had made an even more complex threefold distinction between being '*kultiviert*', being '*zivilisiert*', and being '*moralisiert*' (in the discussion of the Seventh Proposition).

13 J. G. Herder, *Auch eine Philosophie der Geschichte zur Bildung der Menschheit* [1774] (Frankfurt am Main, 1967), 35, 57.

14 *Ibid.*, 45.

15 Cf. Fisch, 'Zivilisation, Kultur', 711.

16 For an excellent recent discussion of the highly complex history of conceptions of the 'nation' (and especially of the 'nation-state') cf. István Hont, 'The Permanent Crisis of a Divided Mankind: 'Contemporary Crisis of the Nation State' in Historical Perspective' in *Contemporary Crisis of the Nation State*, ed. John Dunn (Oxford, 1994).

17 As Michael Forster points out to me, Herder himself uses them in this way in the '*Neunte Sammlung*' of his *Briefe zur Beförderung der Humanität*.

18 Cf. Friedrich von Savigny, '*Vom Beruf unserer Zeit für Gesetzgebung und Rechtswissenschaft*' (Heidelberg, 1814).

19 J. G. Fichte, *Reden an die deutsche Nation*, esp. 'Siebente Rede'.

20 G. Lessing, *Hamburgische Dramaturgie*, esp. 'Zehntes Stück' (2 June

1767), 'Elftes Stück' (5 June 1767), 'Zwölftes Stück' (9 June 1767) and 'Fünfzehntes Stück' (19 June 1767) (all Hamburg, 1769).

21 For Tacitus the 'vigor' of the Germanic peoples wasn't part of a project of imaginary self-aggrandisement in a state of real, vividly experienced political and military debility (as it was for Fichte), but part of the self-criticism of a Roman society still militarily secure and self-confident.

22 Language plays an especially important part in Fichte's discussion of 'primordiality'. The greater etymological perspicuousness of terms for abstract properties in German compared with the Romance languages is taken to indicate a cognitive superiority. The doctrine of the greater primordiality of the German language was one which was to have a long, if not distinguished, career, reappearing in the twentieth century, for instance, in a very vivid form in the work of Heidegger.

23 Cf. end of 'Erste Rede' and 'Elfte Rede'.

24 Cf. 'Zweite Rede' and 'Dritte Rede'.

25 Jakob Burckhardt's *Kultur der Renaissance in Italien* (1860) is an exception to this generalisation and would require treatment in more detail than I can give here.

26 Note that I am *not* making the claim (which I think is false) that there is a 'natural' teleological development culminating in our use of 'culture' and thus that only failure to develop in this direction requires explanation.

27 In one of his last writings Nietzsche claims that *'Kultur'* and the state are 'antagonists' (*GD 'Was den Deutschen abgeht* § 4).

28 'Bismarcks Aussenpolitik und die Gegenwart', *Gesammelte politische Schriften* (Tübingen, 1980), 128. Weber emphasizes the inherent indeterminacy of the concept of 'nation' (Cf. Weber *Wirtschaft und Gesellschaft* [Mohr, Tübingen 1972] pp. 527ff, 242) so this statement doesn't yet definitively settle the question about the relation between culture and the state (the concept of which, Weber thinks, is very clearly defined).

29 Note that, taken out of context, this claim might seem to be ambiguous as between: a) we all agree that, for instance, literacy in *some* language (be it Latin, Old Church Slavonic, or a vernacular) is an essential part of what we mean by 'culture' and only a nation (organized as a state) can provide the extensive public schooling needed to ensure universal literacy; b) we all agree that literacy in the vernacular is an essential part of what we mean by 'culture' and that vernacular will be *the* vernacular of some particular 'na-

tion'; and c) some nations think literacy is an essential element of 'culture'; others think forms of meditation (or religious observance, or cooking and dressing, or whatever) are what constitute 'culture'. So what kind of 'culture' exists will depend on the nation. I'm suggesting that a lot of the early twentieth-century discussions of 'culture' trade on this ambiguity.

30  Cf. Rudolf Haym, *Die Romantische Schule* (Berlin, 1870), 134, 325ff., 375–83.

31  Cf. Immanuel Kant, *Kritik der Urteilskraft*, 1790, and Friedrich Schiller, *Über die ästhetische Erziehung des Menschen in einer Reihe von Briefen* (1793).

32  Kant, *Grundlegung zur Metaphysik der Sitten* (Riga, 1785), 39.

33  Kant has a reply to this line of thought: Although no human could have a 'holy will' we stand under a kind of second-class moral demand (what Kant calls a 'postulate of practical reason') to aspire to approximate the unattainable ideal of holiness of will (*Kritik der praktischen Vernunft* [Leipzig, 1800], 219ff). Cf. also the reply to Schiller in the long footnote of the second edition of Kant's *Religion innerhalb der Grenzen der blossen Vernunft* (Königsberg, 1794), 10ff. Schiller's mistake, of course, was to swallow Kant's doctrine of the moral evaluation of actions whole and then try to fiddle with the details of moral psychology so as to allow room for his preferred views about aesthetics.

34  Schiller, *Über die ästhetische Erziehung*, the last twelve letters.

35  *Ibid.*, 'Dreiundzwanzigster Brief'. Note that Schiller does use *Kultur* here (and in a couple of other places); *Bildung* and *Erziehung* occur constantly throughout.

36  Cf. Schiller's essay *Über Anmut und Würde* (Leipzig, 1793).

37  Marxists see in this ideal of art as the specific realm of free, self-organizing subjectivity a sign of Germany's political backwardness. The West had concrete conceptions, if not of what we could call full political democracy, at any rate of some form of free constitutional political life, but such notions would have been so utopian in nineteenth-century Germany that aspirations to free sociability had to be transferred to the world of art and aesthetic judgment. Cf. Schiller, *Über die ästhetische Erziehung*, 'Siebenundzwanzigster Brief'; also Georg Lukács, *'Zur Ästhetik Schillers'* in his *Probleme der Ästhetik* (Neuwied, 1969).

38  In 1778 Herder published a collection of 'Volkslieder' including a number translated from Slavic languages, although as Konrad Bittner has pointed out (*Herders Geschichtsphilosophie und die Slawen*

[Reichenberg, 1929], 95f.), only four of them are in any sense authentic folk-songs. The last poem in this collection was the 'Klaggesang von der edlen Frauen des Asan Aga' which Herder characterizes as *'Morlackisch'*. The actual identity of the 'Morlachs' (or 'Morlocks') is unclear (cf. B. Gusic, 'Wer sind die Morlachen im adriatischen Raum?' in *Balcanica* 4 [1973], 453ff.), but in this case they must have been South-Slavic-speaking Muslims living in the border area between Herzegovina and Central Dalmatia. This poem is of particular significance because none other than Goethe (using an existing German prose translation by Werthes of the Italian translation published by Fortis in Venice 1774) provided Herder with the verse-version that was printed. Goethe repeatedly expressed his high regard for South Slavic poetry and his cultural prestige at least in German-speaking countries was sufficient to give this judgment significant weight there. The famous fourth chapter of the Sixteenth Book of Herder's *Ideen zur Philosophie der Geschichte der Menschheit* (Karlsruhe, 1784–1791) deals with the Slavic peoples and ends with a direct address to them, predicting their liberation 'from the Adriatic to the Carpathians, from the Don to the Mulde' (this last a tributary of the Elbe, running from south to north between Leipzig and Dresden). Bittner's book cited above deals mainly with the influence of the Slavs on the formation of Herder's philosophy of history. For the influence of Herder on the growth of Slavic nationalisms, cf. Bittner's 'Herders *Ideen zur Philosophie der Geschichte der Menschheit* und deren Auswirkungen bei den slawischen Hauptstämmen' in *Archiv für slavische Philologie* (1929) and Holm Sundhaussen, *Der Einfluss der Herderschen Ideen auf die Nationalbildung bei den Völkern der Habsburger Monarchie* (Munich, 1973). Sundhaussen comes to the not surprising conclusion that the influence of Herder on the actual generation of Slavic nationalisms has been exaggerated. This, of course, is compatible with the view that Herder had an important effect within the German-speaking countries of legitimizing the various Slavic nationalisms. Note also that the Russian Slavophiles in the late nineteenth century were apparently very cool and distanced in their attitude toward Herder because they found in him no support for their claims to a unique superiority of Slavic culture. (Cf. A. Walicki, *The Slavophile Controversy* [Oxford, 1975].)

39 This schema was still very much alive through the 1920s and 1930s as witness the popularity of Thomas Mann's novel *Der Zauberberg* (Berlin, 1924), where the central character, Hans Castorp, a bud-

ding marine engineer from Hamburg, is placed between barbarous Russians who copulate in the morning and let the doors slam and the eloquent Italian rationalist Settembrini. (For the infinitely more witty and melancholy Austrian version of this cf. Robert Musil, *Der Mann ohne Eigenschaften* [Vienna, 1938], Erstes Buch, Erster Teil, chapters 5 and 8.) It is important to qualify views like that expressed by Fritz Stern when he claims that the 'idea of establishing a sharp dichotomy between civilization and culture was born at the time of German Idealism and has played an important and pernicious role in German thought ever since' (*The Politics of Cultural Despair* [Berkeley, 1961], 196, footnote; cf. similar remarks by Norbert Elias, *Über den Prozess der Zivilisation,* Band 1, 7ff.). 'Born at the time of German Idealism' doesn't mean 'developed as a characteristic and integral part of German Idealism' because for Kant the distinction between *Kultur* and *Zivilisation* is not a strictly exclusive one and it is completely different from early twentieth-century versions of this distinction. Hegel's philosophy has no role whatever for any distinction like this, and although Fichte does have the germ of something which later develops in various ways, he doesn't use the term *Kultur* or *Zivilisation* to express it. For further discussion of this cf. Fisch, 'Zivilisation, Kultur', in *Geschichtliche Grundbegriffe,* VII, esp. 681ff.

40 Cf. Hont, 'The Permanent Crisis' in *Contemporary Crisis of the Nation State.*

# 3

# EQUALITY AND EQUILIBRIUM IN THE ETHICS OF ERNST TUGENDHAT

'A NALYTIC' philosophy began to get a toehold in Germany in the early 1970s; a key figure in this process was Ernst Tugendhat, who held one of the chairs in philosophy at Heidelberg (and then later at the Free University in Berlin). Tugendhat's original interests were in epistemology and the philosophy of language (especially discussions of the concept of 'truth'), but during the course of the 1970s he began to work increasingly on ethics. *Vorlesungen über Ethik*[1] is his most substantial and systematic treatment of the subject.

In *Vorlesungen über Ethik* Ernst Tugendhat distances himself from one of the central tasks of moral philosophy in the Kantian tradition, that of giving an absolute grounding or justification for morality. Not only, he claims, can no such absolute or unconditional justification be given, the very idea of an absolute ground of morality is incoherent (*'sinnwidrig'* 79).[2] The apparent need some people seem to feel for 'the absolute' or 'the unconditional' in morality is not something to be taken at face value, but may rather be a breeding ground for decidedly suspicious authoritarian attitudes. At best it is likely to be no more than a residue of experiences from early childhood which we would do better to try to get over rather than use as a guide for philosophizing (87f. 96f). The central component of a morality is a series of propositions or judgments expressing a certain kind of necessity. The central predicate in such propositions is not, as Kant and others have thought, 'should' or 'ought' but 'must' (35–48). 'Ought' and 'should', after all, can characteristically be used in giving people good advice of a non-moral, prudential kind: 'you ought to read that book', 'you ought to eat more vegetables', 'you should get more sleep' etc. The categorical force of morality as we usually conceive of it is better caught by 'must'. 'You ought to get more sleep' but 'you must not lie, kill etc.' Propositions about what I 'must' do, however, although they present themselves as categorical in their force, are meaningful only if there is an immediate answer to the question 'and what if I don't?' and the appropriate immediate response will take the form of the specification of the sanction that will come into effect if I fail to do what I must do (43, 59). Thus 'I must pay my taxes' is meaningful, Tugendhat claims, only if the answer to the counterquestion 'what if I don't?' can be specified ('Her Majesty's Tax Officers will institute legal proceedings against you'). The traditional idea of an 'absolute grounding' for ethics, however, requires either a sanctionless 'must' at the basis of our ethical beliefs – or at any rate a completely free-standing sanction that was the ethical equivalent of a *causa sui* – and since the very idea of such a thing makes no sense, so the traditional project doesn't either. 'Justification' in ethics then, can at best be a process of trying to argue for the plausibility of claims about what I 'must' do by locating these claims in a thickly woven network of reasons, motives, expectations of varying kinds that collectively give the demands of morality a hold on us by at least notionally providing the 'must' of ethics with an adequate sanction (79–89).

Morality for Tugendhat is always a social phenomenon (193). As members of society we make demands on each other; we impose sanctions on anyone who fails to accede to these demands and call those who satisfy them '(morally) good' (56–59). The basic requirement of morality, then, is that we all be cooperative members of society. Tugendhat now claims that the best way to be a fully cooperative member of society – no matter what kind of society that is – is to subject oneself voluntarily to the categorical imperative (80ff.), but holds, contrary to Kant, that the 'justification' for the categorical imperative does not lie in an *a priori* reflective argument about the conditions of the possibility of practical reason, but in series of overlapping and (it is to be hoped) mutually reinforcing (presumably probabilistic) arguments which in the final analysis will appeal (among other things) to complex empirical facts about the nature of human emotions and the demands of human sociability.

There are at least two kinds of questions this line of argument immediately raises. First one might wonder whether the moral good can always be construed as a kind of social cooperation. It is a commonplace about the history of ancient Greece that at a certain point there seems to be a shift to an ethic based on a glorification of the virtues of social cooperation from an earlier heroic ethic based on competition. This is sometimes connected with changes in the military structures with the introduction of 'hoplite warfare' which put a premium on coordination and discipline among men in the line who were 'equally' armed and depended on each other for mutual defense, rather than on the exemplary single-combat which was characteristic of older forms of heroic warfare.[3] 'Heroic' virtue is not unconnected with or completely independent of forms of social cooperation, but it would seem very perverse to claim that for ancient aristocrats being 'good' didn't (at least also or in part) mean being better than others, distinguishing onself (from others) or beating them out in competition. 'Heroic' virtue is not just one more form of social cooperation among others, and so parallel to the egalitarian virtues of the ideally cooperative citizen of the πόλις. Christian saints, too, didn't seem self-evidently always to be instances of the 'good' by virtue of their specifically cooperative properties, at least if those properties are understood relative to any possible terrestrial human society. More mundanely, many social (not just individual) goods demand non-cooperation with real existing communities; examples from the totalitarian societies of the twentieth century come easily enough to hand. If one way

53

of being 'good' is to contribute to the social good, it isn't obvious that the best way to do that is by being maximally cooperative. Perhaps devotees of 'the heroic ethos' and of Christianity are simply wrong about the good, or perhaps one can reconstrue what seem to be non-cooperative forms of behaviour as 'really' in some hidden way 'cooperative', e.g. non-cooperative *vis-à-vis* the actually existing forms of society, but 'cooperative' *vis-à-vis* some imagined ideal society. In any event that case would have to be made; Tugendhat doesn't address these issues.

Second, it is well-known that Kant gives a number of apparently rather different formulations of the 'categorical imperative'.[4] The version of the categorical imperative Tugendhat favours reads: 'Act so that you never use humanity, either in your own person or in that of any other, as a mere means, but always also as an end' (80). This formula is undoubtedly edifying but also more or less completely indeterminate, as Tugendhat realizes, for he tries to go on to gloss the formula first as 'Do not instrumentalize the other' and then as 'Take account (*berücksichtigen*) of the purposes of the other' (146). One might perhaps be forgiven for thinking that even this final version was less than fully specific. What exactly does it mean to 'take account of' or 'take into consideration' others' ends or purposes? Surely not that I do what I think will further those purposes (or what they tell me will further those purposes). Suppose my neighbour is a burglar, a pimp, a drug dealer, or a 'developer'. Do I 'take account' of others' purposes if I put them into my calculation of how to act (but almost always allow them to be outweighed by other factors, for instance my own preferences)? At this point Tugendhat appeals to the notion of 'equality'. I am not taking equal account of others' purposes, if I always allow consideration for them to be outweighed by my preferences. Tugendhat seems to use 'take (equal) account of (all) others' purposes', 'take (all) others into consideration (equally)' and 'respect (all) others (equally)' as rough equiv-

alents, and seems further to assume that we understand sufficiently what is meant by respecting others and taking them into
account. 'Give equal consideration to the purposes of all others'
is his basic ethical principle and he calls his view an 'ethics of
universal and equal respect' (29).

The idea that the demands of morality must bear equally and
in the same way on all people is so deeply entrenched in modern Western societies that we have great difficulty in freeing
ourselves from it even in imagination. The kind of universal
egalitarian morality we naturally accept as the framework for
our moral thinking is by no means the only one that has existed. In many earlier societies it was thought especially important precisely to distinguish between different kinds of people:
slaves and free persons, citizens and non-citizens, those with a
criminal record and those without, women and men, those
who had attained majority and those who hadn't, constituted
distinct classes of people, who did not have the same status,
rights and privileges. It would have been thought a moral mistake to give equal respect, equal consideration, or indeed equal
treatment to members of such self-evidently different groups.
Moral egalitarianism is a fact of modern life; that seems beyond
reasonable doubt. The question is, though, what the standing
of that egalitarianism is, whether convincing grounds can be
given for it, and, if so, what those grounds would be. Is it just a
fact about how we do things, or can we be given some argument, or arguments, to show that this is not just, for instance,
one reasonable way of organizing our moral lives among a
number of possible others, but has some special salience? If it
has such salience, how is that to be understood?

Furthermore, from the fact that we all now in some sense
accept egalitarianism as the unquestioned framework for morality, it by no means follows that there is agreement about
what 'equality' means or how it can best be institutionalized.
Utilitarians hold that the egalitarian ideal would best be realized by the maximization of social utility; in the utilitarian

calculus each person has one vote and all votes have equal weight. That minorities can be consistently outvoted is no objection – only sentimentalists would think it was – but rather an integral part of the proper institutionalization of equality.

Some philosophers (including many who think of themselves as followers of Kant) have disagreed and claimed that all human beings must be seen as the bearers of a set of inalienable human rights which limit the extent to which things can be done to them in the name of increasing the total amount of social utility. These philosophers believe that a system of such equal individual rights realizes the ideal of equality appropriately.

The small group of heretics in the nineteenth century who refused to join in the general chorus of praise of 'equality' included Karl Marx and Friedrich Nietzsche. Oddly enough, given their very considerable differences of opinion on most other matters, Nietzsche and Marx agreed in explicitly and forcefully rejecting the egalitarian ethical ideal. Nietzsche thought that a kind of rudimentary measuring and the comparative weighing up of alternatives, and thus a certain eye for 'equality/inequality' was a very deeply rooted feature of human life – prior, he says, to even the most elementary forms of social life.[5] However, he also thought that *social* egalitarianism destroyed the capacity a society had to generate new values.[6] Since inability to generate new values, what he called 'decadence', was for him about the worst defect a society could have, he was naturally an opponent of equality.

One can trace two strands in Marx's opposition to 'equality'.[7] The first is based on a series of historical claims. Just as a feudal society in which production is based on the hierarchically ordered relations between master and serf secretes around itself an ideological carapace founded on an obsession with 'honour', so for Marx our contemporary obsession with 'equality' is a simple reflection of the alienating demands of the capitalist mode of production.[8] Capitalism subjects all individ-

2. An 'objective' judgment is one that could in principle be affirmed by *anyone*.

3. No one can be expected to agree to a judgment which fails to take adequate account of his or her interests and purposes.

4. That a judgment takes adequate account of my interests and purposes should reasonably be taken to mean that my interests and purposes are considered as much as those of any other person, i.e. that the interests and purposes of all are given equal consideration (80–87; 145ff).

5. Therefore only moral judgments that give equal consideration to the interests and purposes of all have 'objectivity'.

This general way of approaching 'objectivity' (or alternatively 'truth'), namely that 'objectivity' (or alternatively 'truth') is to be *defined* by reference to potential universal agreement, is one that was pioneered, or at any rate popularized, in the later 1960s and early 1970s by Habermas, who seems to have thought he was interpreting C. S. Peirce.[11] It has always struck me as one of the least enlightening fixtures of much recent German philosophy. Obviously for this line of argument to have a chance of getting started, one would have to have a very detailed and plausible account of the *'could'* in the phrase *'could be affirmed'*. One wants to ask *'could be affirmed under what circumstances?'* Specifying these circumstances seems hopeless from the start. It makes things no easier that there is often an unacknowledged shift between *'could be affirmed by anyone'* and *'would be affirmed by everyone'*. I can't pursue this any further here, but suggest that until this rats' nest is untangled, it is appropriate to be skeptical about this whole approach.

Furthermore, Tugendhat himself undercuts the position he has just staked out and provides the conceptual means for seeing that this argument from 'objectivity' won't work. Assuming we accept that this discussion is to be conducted in terms of the concept of 'objectivity', it hasn't yet been proved that 'objectivity' requires that strictly everyone would (or could) affirm the judgment in question. Especially if 'objectivity' just means the opposite of 'arbitrary, merely personal, idiosyncratic', this might be much too stringent a requirement. Perhaps it is sufficient that the judgment in question would be the object of consensus among competent judges (287ff). To use Tugendhat's own example, we might think that the results of a piano competition were in some sense 'objective' if the competition was well conducted, i.e. if certain rudimentary rules of fairness were observed, if the judging was done by a panel of people who had shown themselves to be especially competent, etc. We might deny that such a result was arbitrary, whimsical, idiosyncratic, even though not *everyone* would affirm it. The panel may decide by majority vote, not universal consensus, and after all some humans are tone-deaf or uninterested in music. Not only are the tone-deaf incompetent to judge, but the competent judges have no reason to take account at all of the interests of the unmusical in this context. So perhaps step 2 of the argument needs to be revised to read:

> 2*. An 'objective' judgment is one that would be the majority decision of a panel of competent judges (deciding under conditions that satisfy certain rules of fairness).

To get from 2* to 5 then would require (at least) the further assumption that all humans are competent moral judges. Unfortunately it hasn't been proved that all human beings are competent judges either about questions of morality in general or even of their own (true) interests. After all, Western philosophy in some sense gets started when the Platonic Socrates in *'Protagoras'* and *'Gorgias'* denies that the average Athenian citizen is a competent moral judge. If one wants, therefore, as Tugendhat presumably does, to argue that the ethical principle 'Take equal account of the purposes and interests of all' is not just an expression of our way of doing things – we've settled this for ourselves although it was for Plato a question he still felt the need to discuss – but is 'grounded', it won't do to argue from the assumption that the meaning of ethical judgments requires that they be acceptable to all agents *simpliciter.* To make that assumption comes very close to presupposing a version of the moral egalitarianism the argument was supposed to demonstrate. Tugendhat diagnoses an error of exactly this kind at the heart of Habermas's *'Diskursethik'* (162–169), but variants of the considerations he mobilizes against Habermas tell equally against his own view.

Tugendhat's second argument for moral egalitarianism attempts to show that there can be good reasons and strong motives for any agent to conceive of himself or herself as a subject to whom the demands of universal, equal respect apply and who internalizes these demands. The consistent egoist, Tugendhat admits, cannot be argumentatively refuted (26, 88ff). If I consistently allow my action to be determined exclusively by my momentary impulses and transitory preferences and recognize no external moral authority of any kind, no mere argument will be able to convict me of irrationality or of any other cognitive failing. Nevertheless Tugendhat thinks he can extract from the writings of Erich Fromm a theory of psychic health which will show that any agent should have a strong motive to enter 'the moral world' (63ff). The consistent egoist, who takes account of no one else, will in fact always be suffering from a form of pathological loneliness which can be overcome only by developing an identity of a certain kind: the identity 'member of a moral community'. 'Radical egoism/ morality' is an exclusive alternative, and morality is not like a taxi which will take us just as far as we want and then let us off. It is more like a flight on a scheduled airline, where once the plane has taken off, I can't – unless I wish to try my hand at skydiving – suddenly decide to get out before we have reached our announced destination. Anyone who wishes to overcome loneliness and egoism will have to adopt a thoroughgoingly moral attitude toward other people, but that means always giving equal consideration to the purposes and interests of all others. Psychic health, therefore, requires us to internalize a universal ethic of equal respect.

One might wonder whether 'morality' really must be understood as the kind of monolithic, integrated system proposed here. The argument for the claim that 'radical egoism/universalistic ethic' is a strict alternative is also not convincing. It runs: If one wants to escape egoism, one can't be 'choosy' (*wählerisch*, 93) because 'to the extent to which you are the one who determines to which of your fellow-creatures you will give consideration and to which you will not, you would be using your own discretion (*nach Gutdünken*) to determine who was to be respected and who was not, that is, you would be doing this from your own egotistic perspective' (93). One is tempted to reply to this with a cheery 'So what?' This argument seems to presuppose that the radical extirpation of egoism had value in itself, and that one could coherently speak of a radically non-egotistic form of human action, perhaps one in which God was acting through the purified human soul (and body). Various religious thinkers have made claims of this type. In secular philosophic contexts, however, one would like some reason for these extraordinary claims. Can the metaphysical loneliness which is at issue here really be overcome by accepting the demands of a universalist ethics? Is it even obvious that metaphysical loneliness is always a sign of poor psychic health? Can it be overcome *only* by radical extirpation of egoism? After all, Tugendhat himself admits that less radical measures may be effective against normal everyday socio-psychological loneliness (281). In many countries pubs serve this function. Naturally I will be the one to decide whom I will respect and whose interests I will take account of under what circumstances, just as I would be the one who would decide whether I wish to enter the moral world of universal, equal respect. From the fact

62

that I don't initially decide *a priori* to respect all equally, it doesn't follow that my decision to respect some (but not others) is arbitrary or that I am then simply allowing my momentary impulses to dictate my policy. To the extent to which I am committed to taking systematic account of the interests and purposes of even one other person, I would seem to have left radical egoism behind, without, as far as I can see, in any way having sold my soul to an ethics of universal, equal respect. To claim: 'You must *either* adopt once and for all an ethics of universal, equal respect *or* you will be condemned to a life of complete arbitrariness and egotism' seems to me not so much a constructive development of Fromm's theory, as an instance of the 'fear of freedom' Fromm analysed in his well-known book.[12]

The third attempt to 'ground' an ethics of equality forms part of Tugendhat's discussion of the concept of distributive justice (364 ff.). Tugendhat distinguishes two opposing positions in the debate about the correct way to conceptualize justice: a) an egalitarian conception of justice as 'equal distribution', and b) an 'Aristotelian' conception which holds that justice is distribution *'proportional* to' (or 'relative to') something else, e.g. justice is distribution proportional to merit (373). The egalitarian conception, Tugendhat claims, is characterized by greater theoretical simplicity, because even the Aristotelean

> presupposes the egalitarian conception as the *basis;* the Aristotelean, too, holds that an equal distribution is a just distribution, as long as there are no reasons to depart from it. It is therefore false to try to designate the egalitarian position as the one that must in the first instance justify itself. In itself the egalitarian position requires no justification: the need for justification, the *onus probandi,* lies on the other side. The privileged position of equality results from the fact that it is the simplest rule of distribution'. (374)

I wish to suggest that if one fully appreciates the point Marx makes very forcefully (and with special reference to issues of distributive justice) in *'Critique of "The Gotha Programme"'* (*cf. supra* pp. 56 ff.) that equality and inequality are a *pair* of concepts of reflection that necessarily belong together, and are correlative in their application – *any* distribution will be both equal and unequal – it becomes difficult to see claims about the purported 'greater theoretical simplicity' of equality over inequality as anything other than confusion. One can't break one concept out of such a correlative pair and sensibly claim that it has 'priority' over the other.

The twentieth-century philosopher who has seen this point most clearly and tried most consistently to develop it is Adorno.[13] Most of his discussion is couched in terms of 'identity' not 'equality', but most of the points he makes about 'identity' are transferable. Perhaps the most striking claim Adorno makes is that judgments of 'identity' (and thus, I suggest, also of 'equality') can be seen as located within a social, political, and theoretical apparatus which is geared to *producing* identity – to claim that X and Y are identical is to be engaged in trying to make them more and more alike – and that the existence of such an apparatus is not an unmixed blessing.[14] The apparatus can be used repressively to crush out difference, 'non-identity' (or 'inequality'). In particular, overlooking, or explicitly denying as Tugendhat does above, the 'reflective' nature of judgments of identity/difference (or equality/inequality), virtually ensures in the long run that the apparatus will be used for repression. Hence the necessity of trying to 'rehabilitate' reflection and give both identity and non-identity (equality and inequality) their due.[15] Unfortunately Adorno tends to confuse this perfectly reasonable line of argument with another more radical and less promising one. Namely he sometimes seems to argue not that we should redress the balance between 'identity-thinking' and awareness of difference, but that we should aspire mimetically to represent the non-identical.

Tugendhat's discussion of distributive justice brings to light very clearly his oddly constricted relation to Rawls. Tugendhat himself asserts that egalitarianism requires no special justification, but at the same time complains that Rawls simply presupposes an egalitarian concept of distributive justice (365). I take it that Tugendhat is not objecting to the egalitarian content of Rawls's view, but rather has some reservations about Rawls's method. Tugendhat claims that the method of 'reflective equilibrium' Rawls uses cannot give an adequate grounding for ethics, but can at best reflect and organize our existing moral intuitions, while leaving them finally hanging in the air (25f). Since Tugendhat himself rejects the possibility of an absolute grounding for ethics, it is hard to see what he finds so objectionable about Rawls's method. To translate Rawls procedure,[16] as far as I understand it, into the terminology favoured by Tugendhat, a conception of morality is 'justified' or 'grounded' to the extent to which it is part of the content of a state of equilibrium that has been attained through reflection. Since, as Rawls and Tugendhat agree, 'absolute' justification isn't possible, being 'justified' or 'grounded' will be a question of degree. The 'justification' or 'grounding' is firmer and more secure, the more robust and stable the state of equilibrium attained is. An attained state of equilibrium is the more robust and stable a) the greater the number of elements that have been encompassed in the process of reflection (intuitions, arguments, theories), and b) the freer, more cogent, and more imaginative the process of rendering these elements coherent with each other has been.

I wonder if Tugendhat's rejection of Rawls's method of reflective equilibrium doesn't stem from a misunderstanding on his part of the term 'intuition'. Tugendhat claims that Rawls's method of reflective equilibrium excludes the possibility of a comparison of our intuitions with other sets of theories and intuitions or with the theories and intuitions of other people. 'Intuition' is a highly vague and ambiguous term, but I take it that in Rawls it is being used as part of a contrasting pair: 'intuition/theory'. The original contrast is between two ways of

making moral judgment. I am judging 'intuitively' if I am spontaneously and unself-consciously expressing my immediate
moral judgment of (perhaps we would say, my 'immediate reaction to') an individual case. On the other hand, I am judging
'theoretically' if I am deploying a consciously and explicitly
held set of general propositions which I am willing to defend
argumentatively and deducing from them a moral judgment
about an individual case or a class of cases. Derivately then an
'intuition' is the spontaneous individual judgment I make,
when I am judging 'intuitively' (and a 'theory' is the set of
discursive general propositions I deploy when I am judging
'theoretically'). Finally I can generalize further and use 'intuition' to refer not to a spontaneous moral judgment some individual makes about a particular case, but to the kind of judgments people (in a certain society) habitually or characteristically make about certain kinds of cases.

Obviously the distinction between an 'immediate' or 'spontaneous' judgment and a reasoned, theoretical judgment won't
be hard and fast, and there will be lots of cases that won't fit
easily into one category or the other. I don't see that this is a
particular difficulty as long as the distinction is useful for the
purposes for which it was introduced. Furthermore it is obvious
that 'intuitions' in this sense can and do vary enormously between individuals in the same society and between societies,
and they are also obviously historical magnitudes that change
greatly over time. They arise as a result of the complex interac-
tion of a variety of causal factors. These factors could in principle include economic, social, and political change, the rise and
fall of various forms of religious belief, shifts of population, and
in short any of the myriad of things which form the bread and
butter of the historian. One of the 'historical factors' that may
be responsible for the existence of an intuition, either an intuition some individual has or one that is widespread in a certain
society, may be the existence of a theory. Intuitions may be part
of the residue or historical sediment of theories. When utilitar-

ianism has been around for a few generations, is discussed, written about, taught in the universities, etc. this may eventually come to warp (or, as a utilitarian would see it, 'enlighten') people's spontaneous moral judgments. This doesn't, of course, imply that if I accept a general theory – if tomorrow I decide that utilitarianism is the correct moral theory – , I will immediately find myself equipt with appropriate moral intuitions. In fact, I assume that this is the origin of the whole interest in a distinction between moral intuitions and theories. People are presented with elaborated theories like utilitarianism or Kantianism, armoured at all points. In initial general discussion either one can seem plausible. However, at some point one is likely to begin to try to apply the theories to cases. Then one can be confronted with cases like the one Kant analyses to show that one should never lie even to save someone's life[17] or with one of the more vivid versions of the case about redistributing body parts to increase collective social good that make some utilitarians uncomfortable. Some people, then, will be tempted to say that in their judgment in some cases one *should* lie to save a person's life (or that one ought not to carve up a neighbour even if redistributing his bodily parts would mean a significant increase in overall social utility). They know that this judgment about an individual case does not conform with what the theory prescribes, and they may have no alternative theory which allows them to give an adequate discursive account of why they think that lying might sometimes be permissible or that bodily integrity is an overriding value. 'Intuition' is just the name made up for this kind of judgment which the agent makes despite its incompatibility with some theory which is on offer, and despite the fact that the agent at the moment can offer no alternative theoretical justification for the judgment. Intuitions don't just change, they are also to some extent malleable – within what limits we don't know – , that is we can work at changing them with some hope of success. It is an important fact that we don't know what the limits of malleability are (if indeed there are any), that not all intuitions (at any given time) are *easily* malleable (even if we could in principle *eventually* transform them) and that we generally don't have methods for trying to change our intuitions that are at all effective, reliable or fine-grained, and many of the apparently more effective methods – training up the next generation of young people in a very intense and systematic way – work only very slowly. Intuitions, then, arise and change historically under circumstances and as the result of pressures we can begin to understand (to the extent to which we can understand the origin and development of anything in history); they are malleable, but are not at our disposal. If either of two ways of thinking about ethics and the potential role of intuitions and theories in ethical thought were to be correct, trying to reach reflective equilibrium would be a pointless or hopeless undertaking. First of all, one might deny that mere 'intuitions' had or ought to have any standing in ethical thought at all. What are called 'intuitions' would just be prejudices, and people with 'intuitions' should, as it were, be encouraged to come back when they had got some theories or at least arguments. If we didn't at all have to take account even of very widely held, historically robust intuitions that mattered intensely to the individuals who 'had' them, then we wouldn't, of course, have to try to attain a reflective equilibrium between such intuitions and our theories. It is hard, however, to see how one could adopt this policy of neglect systematically, given that at some point virtually all ethical argumentation will have to deal with the analysis and judgment of individual cases. The second approach that would scotch the project of trying to attain reflective equilibrium would be one that claimed that intuitions were fixed and immutable or, even worse, were 'incorrigible'. If our intuitive judgments were the result of the operation of an infallible or incorrigible faculty of moral insight, then the whole project of trying to educate them and make them compatible with the various theories we develop would be pointless. What we ought to be doing is not trying to get equilibrium between two kinds of items (theories and intuitions), *both* of which are at least in principle changeable, but we should – or rather we must – just stick with our intuitions as fixed points, and try maximally to accommodate any theories we might wish to develop to them. The point of method of reflective equilibrium, however, if I have understood it correctly, is to do two things at once, a) to revise our theories so that they are compatible with our intuitions, and b) to cultivate and educate our intuitions so that they conform with our theories.

This is where I think Tugendhat's error lies. I suspect he thinks that 'intuition' in Rawls means not the sort of thing I have tried to describe above, a relatively unreflective, spontaneous, but in principle variable, individual moral judgment, but rather a Kantian faculty buried in the depths of the human soul which issues fixed, unchangeable, incorrigible moral judgments. Of course if that was what Rawls did mean by 'intuition', one could see why Tugendhat thought Rawls's view excluded the possibility of comparing my intuitions with other people's intuitions and in general made the comparison of different theories with each other seem pointless. If one has incorrigible intuitions, why bother about other people's illusions? Why bother about theories at all? One can also see why Tugendhat would reject that; he is himself very careful to try to discuss as many alternative theories as possible and compare their strengths and weaknesses, and it is perfectly understandable that he would want to object to a view which failed to appreciate the importance of this activity. He is just wrong in thinking that Rawls's method of reflective equilibrium is such a view. The 'reflection' which (if successful) leads to 'reflective equilibrium' will generally have as one important component a comparison of various ethical theories that have been propounded. Even a cursory glance at any of Rawls's published writings will suffice to show that he practices what reflection requires. His misapprehensions prevent Tugendhat from realizing how close he is to Rawls (25, 30).

Tugendhat has very modest views about what philosophical ethics can achieve. 'What we can do in philosophy is no more than render comprehensible our ordinary moral consciousness by analysing its assumptions'(28). Other philosophers have made more ambitious claims for the power of reflection. As has already been mentioned, Tugendhat thinks that Kant's attempt to give an absolute, reflexive grounding of ethics is hopeless (24, 70), and, having despatched the Critical Philosophy, he has equally little time for the 'Critical Theory of Society'.[18] The proponents of the Critical Theory, too, wished to reactivate reflection and bring it to bear on society in a way that went beyond analysing our ordinary moral consciousness. Their ambition, however, was not to justify ethics, but to criticize society. Horkheimer, Adorno, and Marcuse believed that it is impossible to attain a reflective equilibrium in a society like ours. Any more or less well informed and more or less systematically conducted reflection would lead to the conclusion that our normal moral consciousness was so fragmented, disparate, and contradictory that *no* process of mutual accommodation between intuitions, arguments, and theories could ever be expected to end in a state of equilibrium. The reason for this was that our ordinary moral consciousness was just the product of (and thus reflected) an irrational and contradictory form of social and economic life. Capitalism, Horkheimer, Marcuse, and Adorno believed in the 1930s, was an inherently contradictory social formation, and as long as the real contradictions in capitalist society were not abolished, it was fatuous to expect ever to attain a fully coherent and consistent form of ordinary moral consciousness that could be shared by most members of that society. One way of thinking of this is as an expansion of Rawls's method of reflective equilibrium.[19] If Rawls thinks that one must start with our most firmly embedded intuitions, most cogent arguments, and best supported theories and try through reflection to reach a stable state in which (revised versions of) these various components are compatible with each other, the Critical Theory takes very seriously the claim that theories, arguments and intuitions don't stand freely in a realm of their own, but arise out of historical circumstances and in turn influence the course of history. Whether or not one will at all be able to reach a stable reflective equilibrium of the kind Rawls aspires to induce will depend, it is claimed, not just on our ingeniousness in revising our theories and success in educating our intuitions, but in the actual state of society. When one has recognized the role the real state of society plays, however, it becomes obvious that the process of reflection can't *just* be a process of tinkering with our theories and intuitions. If one wants to attain 'equilibrium' that will require changing any social institutions that might systematically prevent such equilibrium from being attained – the Critical Theorists think they have reason to believe that the capitalist form of economic production is one such institution. To show this would be to criticise capitalism.

Tugendhat discusses only one aspect of the Critical Theory and that is its claim to give a criticism of society that was independent of any particular form of philosophical ethics. He develops two objections against this claim. Unfortunately since he misunderstands the essential structural features of at least the version of the Critical Theory that one finds in the writings of Horkheimer and Adorno, both of these two objections completely miss the mark. The first objection runs: In order to criticise a society, one must measure it against certain moral judgments, 'which one must oneself consider to be correct' (6). Thus social criticism presupposes that one can give an account of one's own moral standards. The clarification and justification of moral judgments, however, in the first person, is the task of philosophical ethics. Thus criticism of society is dependent on an antecedent elaboration of a philosophical ethics. As a general line of argument this seems to me false, and it ignores what is one of the central claims of the Critical Theory. It is true that I can try to criticise society by first elaborating and defending my own ethical position and then bringing that to bear on social phenomena. That is one possible way of proceeding; I won't comment on its usefulness as an approach to radical social criticism, but it is also the case that from the very origin of Western philosophy there has also been a completely different model of how to engage in philosophical criticism. This is the form of criticism *more socratico* and it has a completely different structure from the one Tugendhat describes. As a 'socratic' critic I take over 'for the sake of argument' the normative conceptions of the person (or society) in question, without necessarily affirming them or being committed to them myself. The criticism consists in pointing out internal incoherencies and contradictions in these normative conceptions (and associated material). In principle I wouldn't need myself to be committed even to the principle of non-contradiction, provided the person with whom I am arguing (or the society I am criticizing) is committed to that principle. The Hegelian demand that criticism must be 'internal' is a development of this socratic procedure, and the Critical Theory is yet a further development of the same general approach. The proponents of a Critical Theory explicitly claim that what they are trying to do is criticise contemporary society by confronting it with its own contradictions. This project is not unproblematic, but Tugendhat's objection doesn't even engage with it.

Tugendhat's second objection is that the Critical Theory tacitly attempts to give what is in effect a moral criticism of certain normative judgments by pointing out their socio-economic pre-conditions (16). Tugendhat, however, accepts a version of the distinction between factual statements and moral or normative statements, and so believes that no fact one might discover about the actual state of society or about the conditions under which certain normative judgments come to be accepted could have any bearing on the moral standing of such judgments. *Prima facie* the distinction between facts and norms or moral claims does seem to have some plausibility. It might well be the case that we ought not to steal even if we live in a mafia-culture where theft is rife and not even in itself an object of any special social disapproval. However, what plausibility this distinction might seem abstractly to have tends to dissolve in contexts of concrete moral argumentation, and I don't think that this is just because people confronting pressing practical problems often have no leisure to respect nice conceptual distinctions. The distinction exercises the greatest imaginative hold over mind when we consider an isolated individual moral judgment and wonder how any possible configuration of the world could support or confute that judgment. The difficulty here, though, is perhaps less the result of a split between the normative and factual than of the fact that one has begun the exercise with an isolated, individual moral judgment and this is an inappropriate representative of 'the moral' or 'the norma-tive'. Morality is not a collection of disconnected individual judgments – that is, perhaps, by the way, another reason for rejecting certain more extreme forms of intuitionism – but rather we can speak of a human morality in any interesting sense only if there are connections between the concepts used, arguments that purport to join particular claims to other claims, and only if some attempt is made to relate some of the claims to the requirements of human action and forms of human feeling and sociability. At this point the path might seem to fork, the right branch leading off to Hegel and a conception of morality as a more or less unitary whole, ideally like the system of *Sittlichkeit* Hegel believes is realized in modern states, the left curving off in the direction of Nietzsche's claim that moralities in general (and modern morality in particular) are jerry-rigged, non-unitary structures, composed of subsystems that retain a considerable amount of their original independence.[20] Despite some very significant differences between a basically Hegelian and a basically Nietzschean approach, neither one is committed to atomism in studying morality. One can think, then, of moralities as 'systematic' in that the connection between their various parts is important without committing oneself on the issue of whether each morality (or even any morality) is a *single* unitary system. If one decides to proceed in this way, it is less clear that factual claims can play *no* role in the evaluation of the morality as a whole.

To put the point perhaps slightly less abstractly, 'really existing' moralities very frequently make very strong assumptions about the nature of the social world, about (facts of) human motivation, about the likely consequences of acting in one way rather than in another. If a morality prescribes certain kinds of actions and gives as part of the grounds for this prescription some claim about the real world, then obviously showing that that claim about the real world is false in *some* sense can count as a criticism. If the morality in question *systematically* presupposes a set of purported basic facts about the world, and its prescriptions rely on these presuppositions, then showing that the purported facts are no such thing would presumably count as criticism of the morality. By criticising the *morality* in this way I haven't, to be sure, necessarily shown that any individual prescription this morality might make is to be rejected – from the fact that the grounds cited for a particular prescription are false, it doesn't follow that there might not be other, fully adequate reasons for following the prescription – but Tugendhat's focus on the individual moral judgment is in any case not one the proponents of the Critical Theory share. They are not really so concerned with individual moral or ethical judgments, but rather with certain systematic features of wide-spread forms of contemporary morality. The main difficulty here for the Critical Theorists is to make out the case that a form of morality really does 'presuppose' certain factual claims. Often this will require a considerable amount of constructive interpretation, which proponents of the morality in question may well be disposed to reject. Still this seems to have to do with the details of how to make a particular critical argument stick, rather than with some inherent defect in this way of going about social criticism. Note, finally, that none of this implies that the distinction between fact and value is meaningless or even that it is useless in all contexts.

The neo-Kantianism which in the works of Jürgen Habermas celebrates its resurrection from the dead with a great shout and the clatter of many timbrels succumbs to Tugendhat's criticism of the circularity in his attempts to give an 'absolute grounding' for ethics, but the original Critical Theory of the 1930s was anti-Kantian, opposed to all forms of '*Ursprungsphilosophie*',[21] and would have had no more truck with transcendental pragmatics or theories of practical 'discourse' than with the transcendental subject and the *a priori* forms of pure practical reason. In the discussion above I have tried to put the project of the original Critical Theory in a way that is as accommodating to Tugendhat as possible, even at the price of slightly distorting Horkheimer's, Adorno's, and Marcuse's actual views (for instance, by assuming that one can blithely speak, as we do in ordinary parlance, of social 'facts' without analysing in greater detail what could be meant by that). If Tugendhat wished to enter into a discussion of the original form of the Critical Theory, he would have to begin by trying to give some more serious consideration to the strand of ethical thought that starts (as far as we can tell) with Socrates, threads its way through Hegel's ideal of 'internal criticism' and culminates in Adorno.

Tugendhat's modest suggestion that the point of philosophical ethics is to render comprehensible our ordinary moral consciousness is naive, if it implies that he thinks that consciousness is antecedently determinate, coherent, and fundamentally in order and simply needs to be made transparent. It is unlikely to have escaped Socrates' notice that analysing forms of moral consciousness is continuous with criticizing and transforming them; it certainly didn't escape the notice of those who accused him of corrupting the youth. It is one of the great advantages of Rawls's approach over Tugendhat's that he is fully aware of this point and has been able to incorporate it into his philosophical project. The early Critical Theory is just a bit further down this road. It isn't for nothing that Nietzsche, who, in some of his moods, tried to get as far away from discursive philosophical ethics as possible, and who aspires perhaps even to dispense with justificatory thinking in morality altogether, had a fascination with the figure of Socrates, as his only worthy opponent.[22]

### NOTES

1 Suhrkamp, Frankfurt/M, 1993.
2 Numbers in parentheses in the text refer to pages of Tugendhat's *Vorlesungen über Ethik* (Suhrkamp, Frankfurt, 1993).
3 Cf. A. Andrewes, *The Greek Tyrants* (Hutchinson, London, 1956), esp. chapter iii; M.I. Finley, *Early Greece: The Bronze and Archaic Ages* (Norton, New York, 1970) esp. chapters 8 & 11; A. Snodgrass, *Archaic Greece: The Age of Experiment* (University of California Press, Berkeley 1980), esp. chapter 3; W.G. Forrest, *The Emergence of Greek Democracy: 800–400 BC* (McGraw-Hill, New York, 1966).
4 The standard older treatment is H.J. Paton, *The Categorical Imperative* (Harper, New York, 1947).
5 Nietzsche *GM* II. 8
6 Nietzsche *JGB* 'Was ist vornehm?'
7 There is actually a third strand to be found especially prominently in some of the early works which connects the desire for radical equality with forms of envy. Cf. Marx and Engels, *Werke* (Berlin, 1981), *Ergänzungsband I.534f.*
8 Marx and Engels, *'Kritik des "Gothaer Programms"'* in *Werke* (Berlin, 1972) vol. 19, 15ff, esp. 21.
9 Marx and Engles, *Werke*, vol. 3, 423ff.; vol. 23.214ff.
10 Marx, *Werke*, vol. 19, 21f; cf. *Werke*, vol. 3, 425f.
11 Jürgen Habermas, *Erkenntnis und Interesse* (Suhrkamp, 1973), chapter 5.
12 Erich Fromm, *Escape from freedom* (Farrar & Rinehart, New York 1941).
13 Especially in his *Negative Dialektik* (Suhrkamp, Frankfurt, 1966).

14 Adorno, *Negative Dialektik* (Suhrkamp, Frankfurt, 1966), pp. 147ff.

15 Adorno also wishes to overcome the assumption Tugendhat seems to make that in an ethical controversy one 'side' will always have the *onus probandi*. The *onus probandi* will always be taken to lie with those who wish to change the status quo, Adorno thinks, so setting up the discussion in this way builds into it a conservative bias.

16 John Rawls, *A Theory of Justice* (Harvard, 1971) § 9; cf. also Rawls, *Political Liberalism* (Columbia University Press, 1993), esp. pp. 90–8.

17 I. Kant, *'Über ein vermeintliches Recht aus Menschenliebe zu lügen'*.

18 For an excellent introduction and overview cf. David Held, *Introduction to Critical Theory* (University of California Press, 1980).

19 Obviously I don't mean to suggest that historically the procedure used by the Critical Theorists arose as a generalization of Rawls's method of reflective equilibrium, since the canonical works of the Critical Theory were written in the 1930s, drawing on a tradition of theorizing that went back into the nineteenth century; Rawls published nothing until well after the Second World War

20 Cf. 'Nietzsche and Morality' *infra* pp. 167–71.

21 Cf. Adorno, *Zur Metakritik der Erkenntnistheorie* (Kohlhammer, Stuttgart, 1956), *'Einleitung'*.

22 Nietzsche, *GD 'Das Problem des Sokrates'*.

# 4

## ART AND THEODICY

I N this essay I would like to consider a strand of thought about art that was influential in Central Europe during the nineteenth and early twentieth century. This is a strand which attempts to see art as in some sense 'cognitive' and connects it very closely with religious and theological concerns, especially with the kind of concern that gives rise to the discipline of philosophical theology called 'theodicy'. Although there are some anticipations of this approach in Kant, especially in his doctrine of beauty as the symbol of morality, and also in various early Romantics (including, notably, Schelling), I will begin with a discussion of Hegel's views, because he seems to me to pose the issue in a way that is philosophically fully developed and which has had a continuous history of influence from the time it was originally proposed. Unfortunately Hegel's views are both very complex and so integrated that it is hard to isolate any part for separate consideration, so I must begin by taking a step backward and expounding some of general features of his philosophic approach that one needs to understand to follow his account of art.

When Aristotle[1] speaks of the origin of philosophy in 'wonder' (θαυμάζειν), I take it that the tacit affect he had in mind as the natural concomitant of this 'wonder' was that of a fascinated admiration of what is so remarkable as not to be immediately comprehensible. The story was told in the ancient world that the athlete Myron walked into the stadium one day carrying a newborn calf. Each day he repeated this performance and each day the calf grew bigger and heavier until finally Myron

78

came into the stadium carrying a full-grown cow. If I see Myron walk into the stadium carrying a weight that seems impossibly heavy, e.g. a full-grown cow, I may experience a generous feeling of pleasure at the spectacle – '*how marvelous*' – and may be drawn to keep watching it, but may also have a need to understand how it is possible. I may try out various explanations – Myron comes from a family that has long been known for producing good weight-lifters and so is a thoroughbred; Myron eats a special diet no one else eats; Myron trains in a special way; Myron is inspired or possessed by a god (or a god has actually taken Myron's place); the whole thing is a fraud because the 'cow' has been tampered with. . . . There is, Aristotle would then be suggesting, a natural progression from 'how can he lift *such a heavy* weight?' to 'how is it that eels *always* beget other eels (and not e.g. cows)?' to 'how is the One related to the Many?'

Some philosophers, however, have claimed a different origin for philosophic speculation. They have thought that philosophy (and religion) arise out of a certain kind of strongly negative affective human experience, an encounter with the world as radically defective, disappointing, or unsatisfactory. Children and reflective adults who look around their world will find much of what they see painful, absurd, or revolting. Thus Prince Gautama, brought up in an artificial environment where everyone was young and healthy, is shocked by his first encounter with old age, sickness, and death, and this shock and revulsion may give way to a sense of puzzlement and a need to understand how such things are possible (and what, if anything, can be done about them). If our reaction to Myron is: 'That is much *better* than I expected; how wonderful!', Gautama's reaction to what he sees outside the royal compound is: 'That is much *worse* than I expected; how awful!'

Historically there have been a number of variants of the second, Prince Gautama's negative, reaction. In some versions emphasis will be put on the deficiencies of the world; in others on our own failings.[2] Some versions will focus on the cognitive dimension – difficulties we might have in seeing the world as comprehensible, rational, meaningful, coherent – , others on the more strictly moral or psychological issues – the failure of the world to conform to our moral standards or to be amenable to the realization of our desires and interests. If, then, philosophy arises from the experience of a discrepancy between what we are very vividly forced to see *is* the case and what we think in some sense 'ought' to be the case, between reality and expectation, then success in the philosophical enterprise could come about in at least two possible ways: either philosophy could show us that contrary to first appearances reality does conform to our expectations – the wicked really are punished for their wrong-doing in some recognizable sense of the word 'punish', although the punishment takes place in ways that are not immediately evident – , or it could show us that (and ideally, how) we can and should change our expectations to accommodate reality.[3] In more interesting versions *both* of these processes are thought to take place together. Thus in certain forms of Christianity, the claim is made that the wicked *are* punished, so the moral economy of the world is vindicated, but also that the nature of the 'punishment' is sufficiently different from what we might antecedently have understood as 'punishment' (e.g. deprivation of the Beatific Vision) that we are required to change the standards we use for judging when the world can be said to be morally in order.[4]

Hegel is best understood as a philosopher who stands in the second of the two traditions outlined above. As human beings[5] we have a fundamental – in fact Hegel calls it an 'absolute' – human need to be genuinely 'at-home' (either *'zu Hause'* or *'bei sich'*) in the world, where 'the world' includes not just the natural universe, but also the social, cultural and political world in which we live.[6] We usually use the term 'need' in a relative way, with reference, at least tacitly to some other purpose to which the thing I 'need' contributes essentially. If I say I need something it usually makes sense to ask what I need it *for*. I may need another nail to hammer down the roof of the potting shed firmly, or a new tyre so that I can use my bicycle again, or more time to finish a project, or a continuing supply of fresh water so that I do not suffer from thirst. Hegel claims that the need to be at-home in the world is 'absolute' in that it is not relative to any other set of possible human purposes. We humans want to satisfy this need for its own sake, i.e. just because we are human and it defines what it is to be human. We can't find any purposes outside itself to which the satisfaction of this need contributes or give any reason for trying to satisfy this need that wouldn't eventually be circular, i.e. that could be fully specified completely independently of reference to the absolute need itself. This absolute need gives rise to an associated set of expectations about how the world 'ought' to be, a set of expectations that aren't automatically satisfied in human life as we know it. Especially in more complex human societies humans will easily fail to find their social world comprehensible or will feel alienated from it. Oddly enough, then, being 'at home' in our world, although part of what we absolutely need, is not, at least for inhabitants of the 'modern world',[7] our 'natural' state, i.e. it isn't the state we would find ourselves in if we, as it were, failed to exert ourselves. Philosophy, art, and religion are for Hegel all forms of what Hegel calls 'absolute spirit'; they are, he thinks, just various ways of trying to satisfy our absolute need.

For this absolute need to be fully satisfied at least two conditions must be fulfilled. First of all, it must actually be the case that the world we live in (including our social and political world) *is* basically rational, comprehensible in principle, and 'commensurate' to us in the sense that it is amenable to allowing us to realize our deepest human interests and aspiration. Obviously it is the very opposite of a trivial task to ensure that this condition is met. Thus, Hegel believes, no society that allows slavery can be one in which humans can genuinely be 'at-home' because its basic institutional structure is one that thwarts some of our deepest human aspirations. In fact, only since the French Revolution and the ensuing, incipient institutionalization of the idea that human political life should be directed at attaining a specifically modern kind of rational social freedom has our political and social world become 'commensurate' to us to a sufficient extent to allow us to be at-home in it to any appreciable degree.[8]

On the other hand, once we have eaten of the fruit of disappointment with our world or ourselves – and, given history and what it is to be human, we have all in one way or another done this – it won't be enough to satisfy our absolute need that the world just *is* in order and 'good', but something must show or make visible or represent (*darstellen*) to us that our world is good, rational, comprehensible etc. For us an integral part of being at-home is coming to *see* that we are at-home. As Hegel puts it, to be at-home for us requires that we have been 'reconciled' to our world; philosophy, religion, and art are three ways of trying to attain that reconciliation.[9]

One great stumbling block to our attempts to be reconciled with the world is the existence of evil, which seems to be a feature of our world that we can't do away with by any non-utopian transformation of our political and social world. Christianity was faced with the problem of how to understand the existence of evil in an especially vivid form, given that it also believed that the world and everything in it was the creation of an omnipotent and benevolent diety. 'Theodicy' in the strict sense is the name for that theological discipline which attempts to show that the existence of evil is compatible with the claim that the world was created by a benevolent and omnipotent god. Hegel takes over the term 'theodicy' from Christian theology but construes it in a somewhat more encompassing sense than the narrowly religious one in which it had its origin.[10] For Hegel the full task of theodicy is not just to 'solve' the 'problem of evil' but to discharge the whole programme of showing us that our absolute need for reconciliation with the world as a whole, as described in the last few paragraphs, was satisfied. To give a successful 'theodicy' in this sense is the central goal of philosophy, art, and religion.

If one really can distinguish, as I have above, two conditions that must be satisfied for there to be a fully satisfactory theodicy, namely that

a) in a world that *is* basically rational, good, and commensurate to us,
b) the 'theodicy' shows us that (a) is the case

then this suggests that we might countenance the possibility of a deceptive or false theodicy. Such a theodicy would be one which presented a world in which our deepest interest weren't and couldn't in fact be satisfied *as if* it were one in which we were at-home. This depends on taking 'show' in (b) above in a merely phenomenological sense – to give an appearance which in fact persuades us without any commitment to the ultimate truth or well-groundedness of the appearance in question.[11] A 'true' theodicy,[12] by contrast, would be one with reference to which we could take 'show' to mean '*correctly* exhibits'. . . . Obviously, then, a true theodicy would be possible only if our world is fundamentally 'in order'. Since, as has been mentioned, this is, for Hegel, not the case through the whole of human history up to the French Revolution, theodicy in the full Hegelian sense (i.e. attempting to give a 'true' theodicy) is a hopeless undertaking for most of human history. From the fact that the revolution establishes the basic principle that society should be rationally organized so as to realize universal freedom and sets out to implement this project, it doesn't follow that the revolutionaries actually had a complete, correct, and perfect understanding of what this would imply, or that the correct principles were fully diffused throughout society and society totally restructured so as to embody them. Much less does it follow that everyone who lives in the post-revo-

lutionary society correctly understands that it is now appropriate to be 'reconciled' to society (in a way in which it would not
have been appropriate to be reconciled to feudal society).[13] The
'moment' of Hegel's philosophy is precisely the moment between the Revolution – the clear enunciation of the right principles in the context of an effective historical process of imple-
menting them fully – and the (prospective) final embodiment
of those principles in what Hegel thought was their most adequate and appropriate form, that of a fully developed bourgeois
society with the political structure of an organic but constitutional monarchy. Because post-revolutionary society is fundamentally rational and good – the right principles are publicly
recognized and are in the process of being fully implemented –
condition (a) above is satisfied and 'true' theodicy is possible;
because the process of construction of the fully free and rational society is not yet complete and because people still cling
to old-fashioned abstract conceptions, philosophy is needed
and has an important social role to play both in guiding the
constructive activity and in 'reconciling' people to that task and
the world that is coming into being through it.

A fully successful theodicy of the kind to which the forms of
absolute spirit (i.e. art, religion, and philosophy) aspire, then,
will be both true and convincing. Before the Revolution,
though, i.e. through most of human history, religion, philosophy, and art had an uncomfortable choice to face. Since the
world (at any rate the social and political world) wasn't in
order, the forms of absolute spirit could either tell the truth
about it – that it was irrational and incommensurate to the
realization of our deepest interests – but that would mean failing to give the (successful) theodicy which it was in their nature to aspire to provide, or they could give a false theodicy,
comforting illusions, but that would be no more than another
kind of failure.[14]

There are at least two aspects of the account I have given so
far of Hegel's conception of a 'theodicy' that might seem to

require further comment. Recall that the 'absolute need' out of which philosophy, religion, and art arose was said to be a need to see the world as a place in which our deepest human interests could be satisfied. First of all, one might wonder about the relation between our 'absolute human need' and our 'deepest human interests'. Is a need the same thing as an interest, and is our 'absolute' need the same as our 'deepest' interests? Hegel doesn't have an official systematic distinction between 'needs' and 'interests', but he does clearly differentiate between what he calls our 'absolute' (or 'rational' or 'highest') need and various contingent, relative, accidental or otherwise adventitious 'needs' people might at various times develop.[15] I wish to claim, though, that Hegel's discussion suggests that we can think of the 'absolute human need' for reconciliation as something singular and transhistorical – it is a need to be at-home in the world which can in some sense be discerned as the same throughout human history – and that in contrast to what will count as 'our deepest human interests' will change and develop through time (although, Hegel thinks, not in a random way but in a way which can itself be seen, at least from its final point, as having a rational, and indeed 'absolute' structure). At any rate I will adopt that terminological convention. So 'our deepest interests' will mean something like 'whatever are the deepest interests of the people of that historical time'.[16] I will further assume that these 'deepest interests' have the same kind of autotelic property Hegel attributes to our 'absolute need', i.e. these 'interests' designate things that are taken to be ends in themselves. So, both in the ancient world and in the modern world we can see people trying to satisfy their absolute need to be at-home/reconciled with their world. This means in both cases trying to see their world as accommodating their deepest interests. However, in each case what the deepest interests are is something different. Thus in the ancient world people's deepest interests will have to do with attaining political control of their collective life in the public world; in modern times,

however, Christianity adds a dimension of interiority and subjectivity to human life. Politics alone won't be enough and
people's deepest interests will encompass at least to some extent an interest in the satisfaction of various demands for individual happiness, for an acceptable constitution of their private
life, etc.[17] This means that the absolute need of humanity will
(always) be to see the world as the kind of place within which
their deepest interests (whatever they historically are) can be
realized.

It is further the case that we won't always be consciously and
explicitly aware either of our absolute need or of our deepest
interests. It is reasonable to assume then that an important part
of satisfying our absolute need will be making us more clearly
aware of what our interests are, 'bringing them to consciousness' if only because it might be thought to be difficult to see the
world as amenable to the realization of our deepest interests, if
we didn't know what these were.

This immediately raises the issue of the cognitivity of the
forms of absolute spirit, especially art. It is in general clear that
Hegel holds that art is a kind of knowledge and that significant
art in some sense presents us with truth, but it is extremely
difficult to say exactly what this means. At first glance it might
seem that Hegel shifts uncertainly between claiming:

a) that art depicts a quasi-object (called 'The Divine', 'The
   Absolute', 'The Truth') – it would be easy to connect this
   with Hegel's obvious assumption that the archetypical
   form of art is a representation of a god (in the form of a
   statue, or picture)[18]
b) that (significant) art expresses a truth.[19]

This looks like a vacillation between what old-style epistemology might have called two different conceptions of knowledge,
one that took it as a kind of acquaintance (*connaître, kennen*),
and one that construed it as propositional (*savoir, wissen*). In the
first sense art would be 'cognitive' in that it would make me

acquainted with something in the way in which, for instance, I might become acquainted with Marcel or with the Branden-burg Gate by looking at photos or paintings, or with the city of Berlin by studying a map. *What* I came to be acquainted with (roughly, God) was, to be sure, an odd object, but that might be the fault of the object, not of the account of what it meant to know it. On the second conception art would be called 'cogni-tive' because in coming properly to understand a work of art I would learn something like a propositional truth, e.g. (if the work in question was a statue of a Greek god) that human and divine natures were not radically different the one from the other. It will, of course, be immediately evident to anyone with even a passing knowledge of Hegel's general position that nei-ther of these two possibilities can really hope to be an adequate interpretation. 'The Absolute' is very clearly not anything like an object (or person) that could be 'known' in the first sense, and Hegel is very clear that garden variety propositional truths are fine for the realm of everyday life, but have no place in the domain of 'absolute spirit'. The central items of philosophy are what Hegel calls *'speculative* propositions'; these are momentary expressions of a certain complex movement of thought and not equivalent to ordinary propositions or sets of such proposi-tions.[20] Neither (a) nor (b) above would in turn seem self-evidently to be the same as the view, which Hegel seems also to hold,

(c) that art makes us aware of our deepest interests.[21]

Obviously 'make us aware of our deepest interests' is to be interpreted to mean 'makes us have *correct* awareness of (what are truly) our deepest interests'. I can normally be said to have become aware of various things without it necessarily being the case that I can formulate that awareness in a proposition, and awareness of an interest, whatever it finally turns out to be, seems also rather different from acquaintance with an object or person. I will return to the question of the cognitivity of art later, but for the moment I wish to hold fast just the claim that it is central in understanding art to see it as helping to satisfy our absolute need by making us aware of our interests. Note that this should, if the previous account is correct, be only half the story. First I should come to realize what my deepest interests are, *then* also that they can be realized in the world as I find it.

That brings us to the second aspect of my account of Hegel's project that may seem to require further elucidation, namely what exactly does Hegel think can be demonstrated about the possibility of realizing our interests in the world as we find it? There seem to be at least three slightly different possible theses here:

a) weakest thesis: the world isn't (metaphysically) set up so that it will systematically thwart our deepest interests.
b) strong thesis: the world is actually set up so as (on the whole) to foster the realization of at least most of our deepest (rational?) interests most of the time.
c) strongest thesis: the world is metaphysically constituted so that the realization of our deepest human interests (eventually) is virtually *ensured*.

Note that although I have called (a) the weakest thesis, it isn't by any stretch of the imagination trivial, and some philosophers, notably Schopenhauer, have denied it. Schopenhauer, it will be recalled, thought he could argue convincingly that given the kind of creature we humans were with the desires we would naturally have, one could see that our desires would be systematically frustrated and thwarted by the world. Schopenhauer couches his argument in terms of 'desires' rather than 'interests' but it is hard to see how our deepest interests could be realizable if the world really did systematically frustrate our desires. Hegel, as is well known, opts for the strongest version (c), although the historical dimension his gives to the claim (*'eventually'*) may seem to take back – at least for those who lived before the French Revolution – with one hand what it seems to give with the other. 'Now' at any rate (i.e. in the early nineteenth century in Central Europe), Hegel believes, the 'reconciliation' a successful theodicy gives wouldn't just be a grudging agreement that the world is the best we can expect, but rather will create what he calls *'ein wärmerer Friede mit der Wirklichkeit '* than that.[22]The final result of a theodicy is to show us that life as we know it in our world is inherently worth living; this satisfaction of our absolute need should generate in us an affectively positive optimism.

It is in this context that one must see Hegel's philosophy of art. His account has two parts:

A. All art has as its inherent teleological goal to provide us with a true, adequate theodicy, that is:

    a) to bring is to a correct awareness of what our deepest interests are

    b) to show that these interests are realized (or at any rate realizable)

    c) thereby to satisfy our absolute need for reconciliation

    d) to show us that our attitude toward the world ought, therefore, to be one of optimism

B. The essential means by which art tries to attain this goal is a configuration comprising three components:

    a) art has to do with works that are objects having a 'common external existence' (*'ein Werk von äußerlichem, gemeinen Dasein'*)[23]

    b) the work of art is the product of the activity of a human artist, what Hegel calls *'das produzierende Subjekt'*[24]

    c) art-works have sensible properties which are perceived by a 'worshipping'subject (an *'anschauendes und verehrendes Subjekt'*)[25] who is a member of a community of such subjects

Only when all three elements of B above come together so as successfully to attain the appropriate goal (A above) does one have an instance of 'art' in the full sense. Religion and philosophy share the same goal as art (A above) but differ in the means they employ (B above).

That all three of the elements in B must be present for art in the full sense to exist means that for Hegel 'art' is an essentially social and quasi-religious phenomenon.[26] It isn't just an accident that B/c speaks of a community of 'worshippers' as an essential part of art in the full sense. His tacit paradigmatic work of art is the sculpture of a god which is created by human hands (and known to be created by human hands) and which is set up in a public temple to serve as the central point of various cult-practices – perhaps it is dressed in robes, anointed with oil or butter, carried around in procession, spattered with sacrificial blood or taken down to the shore to be ritually washed.

In Hegel's wider philosophical scheme 'beauty' is not really a central category. To be sure, his general philosophic attitude is one of trying to be as all-encompassing as possible, i.e. finding a place in his system for everything, especially for phenomena or categories that have been historically significant, but one must distinguish between what is a constituent driving part of Hegel's own conceptual apparatus and what he tries 'also' to accommodate because he wishes his own view to be systematically and historically exhaustive. Hegel himself (i.e. outside office hours) had neo-classicist views about beauty, as harmoniousness of sensible appearance (*'Schein'*), and he does find a place for a theory of 'beauty' (as the *'sinnliches Scheinen der Idee'*)[27] in his System, but what is really important for him is the satisfaction of our need for reconciliation. Whatever sensible forms contribute to such reconciliation at a given historical time will be the forms that figure prominently and significantly in the art of that period. In some historical periods the tasks of art will be discharged by works that do not present a *'schöner*

*Schein,'* that lack any of the purely sensible harmonious appearance he associates with 'beauty' in the proper sense.

This general approach implies a devaluation of the strictly 'aesthetic', that is of the attempt to understand art through an analysis of the experience of an (individual) human subject, and of the formalist theories of art which are a characteristic of the Kantian tradition. It isn't necessarily that there is no specific individual experience of the beautiful. The work of art must have sensible properties (B/c above), and, of course, the agents involved in collective cultic practices will have complex experiences that will perhaps be in some ways different from normal experience, but what is important is the unitary (social) phenomenon sketched in B/a through c. So there may well be specific forms of sensible experience that are characteristic of (the experience of) 'art', but these will be subordinate components of a larger whole. They won't themselves be fully and correctly comprehensible except by reference to their position in that whole. Furthermore one may not be able to get to what is philosophically most important about art through analysis of the way individuals 'experience' the statue. 'The aesthetic' is a one-sided abstraction from the full phenomenon of art, and any attempt to try to break individual 'aesthetic' experience out of its wider social context and try to base a theory of art on it alone is doomed to result in a failure to understand art.

Art is a form of 'absolute spirit'. As such it is for Hegel autonomous, autotelic, and cognitive, but non-discursive.[28] It is also 'beyond' morality – it isn't concerned with issuing imperatives (hypothetical or categorical), telling us what we 'ought' to do, or with any of the appurtenances of the attempt to boss people around.[29] It doesn't tell us what kind of life we 'ought' to live, but to show us that the life we are living is inherently worthwhile, worth living for its own sake. Part of what it means to say that our life is worth living is that ours is a life of spirit, that is one in which art figures prominently. As a 'justification' this might seem circular – art shows us that life is worth living because it contains art – but Hegel presumably thinks that in discussion of what is worthwhile 'for its own sake' such circularity is unavoidable and no objection. In showing us its own inherent worthwhileness (and thus the worthwhileness of the form of life in which it is embedded) art gives us a kind of 'knowledge', but not one that can be reduced to a proposition or a set of propositions. A work of art (or art in general) doesn't have a detachable moral or make a propositional statement.

Art is for Hegel a human necessity, but also a necessary failure. It is a necessity because we humans are not forms of disembodied *Geist,* but finite beings living in a world of sense. Thus *part* of what it would be for us to become fully reconciled would be to see even this sensible world as not utterly alien to us, and art is the specific way in which that component of the project of reconciliation is discharged. On the other hand, Hegel believes art is a necessary failure because he believes that the means it must employ if it is to remain art (B above) are inherently incapable of allowing it fully to attain its appropriate goal (A above). There is a contradiction built into the very idea of art – art *must* be a failure because it tries to do something that can't be done with the means it is committed to trying to use (if it wishes to remain art). The modern world is highly complex and understanding it requires the use of highly abstract forms of theoretical reason. What we would have to be *shown* in order to recognize what our deepest interests in this world are, and how they can be realized, is too complex, and too abstract ever to be expressible in a work of art, which by definition must be a sensible work (in an appropriate social context). Crudely: a statue of a Greek god, in its appropriate religious and social context, can make people in the ancient world aware of a congeniality between human and divine natures and thus contribute to making them reconciled to the visible world around them with its pleasure and pains, no different in principle from those of the gods. It is not part of the task of art – or at any rate it is not a task that art could conceivably discharge – to try to specify discursively or to analyse theoretically what that 'congeniality' is exactly. (Christian theology tries to do this, but theology is not art.) We, contemporary philosophers, i.e. philosophic readers of Hegel contemporary with him and all those who come later, can look back at ancient art and try to express what was happening there in a way that is sharper and more articulated than any the participants in that artistic culture could have formulated. In participating in art the ancients were being brought to realize: If even the gods have a human shape and live a life not essentially different from that of humans, how bad can it be to be a human? I've consciously put a question here in place of a direct statement. Hegel's claim is that this whole complex (ancient art) may be said to be a form of cognition, even though what it is cognition *of* can't be put in a simple, single, affirmative proposition.

No matter how beautiful and how lovingly tended by its worshippers, though, a statue or painting *can't*, as long as it remains a work of art, really make us aware, for instance, of the deepest interests we moderns have as members of civil society and present the lives we lead as members of such a society as inherently worthwhile.[30] That requires a conceptual and theoretical analysis which can express the more complicated, abstract truths, truths that can't be rendered *visible* but that would need to be expressed for a full theodicy to be successful. Beauty can be the closest approach people in a spiritually inadequate and underdeveloped state of society (one which even tolerates slavery) can get to 'reconciliation', but it is in fact at best a crude first approximation to a theodicy. To be reconciled to our modern world (which is the world in which spirit is most fully and adequately developed) thus requires the deployment of abstract, discursive, theoretical 'means', i.e. philosophy. We may hope, Hegel claims, that art will continue to thrive and develop, to 'advance and perfect itself'[31] in the modern world. Presumably this means that works of art will continue to be produced and that there will be various technical advances – we shouldn't expect art to die off as, for instance, polytheistic religions died off at the end of the ancient period. Art 'in its highest vocation', however, i.e. as that to which we look for giving us an understanding of our deepest interests and reconciliation with our world, is for modern people a thing of the past,[32] and is to be supplanted by philosophy. It isn't, of course, that philosophy now replaces art's attempted mode of sensible demonstration of the worthwhileness of a form of life with a simple propositional truth or collection of such truths, because philosophy doesn't deal in this currency either. For Hegel, philosophy is a continuous, in fact infinite, process of reflective argumentation in which any individual proposition or set of propositions is no more than an idealized position, a geometric point on the itinerary through which reflection moves. Taken out of this process, isolated and fixed, a proposition is a mere *caput mortuum.*

The situation for art is, then, perhaps less dire than first appears. It is in a sense no serious objection to art for Hegel that it is based on a contradiction and thus that any work of art must be a necessary failure. For Hegel in one sense *everything* in the world, including even presumably the Protestant religion (although he is careful not to make this too explicit), is contradictory and a necessary failure; everything, that is, except the final philosophical process of understanding that and exactly how everything is a necessary failure. In some sense the outcome of Hegel's theory is to show us that nothing in the world is any the worse for being in some sense ultimately contradictory and a necessary failure, provided one understands its appropriately limited place in the overall philosophical process which is his System. The philosophical life was really the one that was worthwhile for its own sake, but philosophy itself was a process of speculative reflection on (and that means, to some extent in) an existing form of historical human social life, and art will necessarily be part of such a human social life, although not (any more) the 'highest' part.

Still in the face of this Hegelian account two strategies immediately suggest themselves for trying to give a slightly more upbeat account of the future prospects of art. Roughly speaking, this means denying component A or component B of the schema I presented above. The first is to deny that art must be teleologically directed toward giving a theodicy and suggest ways in which art could actively embrace the absence of what Hegel calls its 'highest vocation', i.e. try in some way to make a virtue out of what Hegel presents as a failure. The second strategy is to question whether all three of the elements in B of Hegel's analysis of the necessary 'means' art employs really are in any sense *essential* features of art. One historically particularly significant line of development here is the denial that art must be *restricted* to 'sensible', i.e. strictly non-conceptual means. If it is wrong to understand art abstractly and one-sidedly relative merely to a particular kind of experience individuals have, but the whole social and cult dimension must be added, why can't one go further and add conceptual and theoretical components? One of the reasons the early German Romantics gave for thinking that the novel was the appropriate form of art for the modern age was precisely that they thought it could accommodate the conceptual and discursive elements that would be needed to give a comprehensive 'view' of the modern world.[33] Literature in general for Hegel is not the paradigmatic kind of art because works of literature don't have the sheer substantial external existence that a building, a painting or statue has; rather literature is the point at which art begins to dissolve itself into a kind of discursivity that will very soon undermine its claims to absolute importance. The novel for Hegel is so unimportant as to be virtually invisible.[34] The question is whether this Hegelian view is not just a prejudice.

Art as a phenomenon, then, for Hegel is deeply ambiguous. On the one hand, it is inherently committed to fostering a certain kind of optimism and affirmation. On the other hand, art is always a necessary failure in a number of different ways.

Art can satisfy the highest need of humans only in relatively primitive historical and social circumstances in a political and social world that doesn't really deserve to be the object of full-fledged reconciliation and affirmation. On the other hand, to the extent to which the world we live in does deserve our affirmation, we can't come to a proper representational reconciliation with it through art because art is, for Hegel, too bound up with that which is given to sense.

Adorno is very adamantly resistant to any attempts to use the first of these two strategies. He thinks it terribly important to maintain the link of art with what Hegel called its 'highest vocation', with the project of making us aware of our deepest interests and of what a worthwhile human life would be, and of telling the truth and giving a fully adequate 'theodicy'. If one gave up that reference to the highest vocation, art would degenerate into mere entertainment.[35] What's wrong with entertainment? We shall see in a moment.

Hegel, then, according to Adorno, asked the right question about art: what contribution can it make to theodicy? But he got the wrong answer. Hegel thought the post-revolutionary world was basically rational and good; Adorno is convinced that the modern world is radically and pervasively evil and irrational. Just as traditional (affirmative) theodicies couldn't really convincingly attain their goal simply by pointing to individual instances of goodness or rationality, so neither is it sufficient for Adorno simply to point to Auschwitz in support of his negative theodicy. Still the example is sufficiently horrible that simply citing it doesn't seem completely lacking in persuasive force. The modern world, Adorno believes, is characterized by a systematic discrepancy that exists between our technical capacities, which are sufficient to turn the whole world into 'paradise' and the actual catastrophic state in which we live (of which Auschwitz is just one of the more vivid and extreme instances).[36] Auschwitz wouldn't have been possible without a high level of development of the forces of production and of technical control over the world, and the fact that it occurred at a historical period and in a place which was technologically highly advanced makes it all the more horrible. It is the discrepancy between technical capacities and the actual use of those capacities and the fact that this discrepancy is, Adorno believes, not merely accidental, but systematic, that constitutes the radical evil of our world. In a way all of Adorno's work (especially the *Dialektik der Aufklärung* which he wrote in California in the 1940s jointly with his friend Max Horkheimer) is a tacit attempt to give further substance to his claim that our modern world (the world of technology, parliamentary democracy, and capitalism) is radically evil, just as all of Hegel's work is in some sense an attempt to demonstrate the necessary progress of reason. Although Adorno occasionally appeals to a version of the Marxist claim that the modern world is evil because it is capitalist, his considered opinion is clearly that capitalism is merely a superficial consequence of a more deep-seated defect. This is a defect in what Adorno (and his collaborator Horkheimer) call 'The Enlightenment' and its associated notion of reason. In Adorno's usage 'Enlightenment' (*Aufklärung*) doesn't refer just to a particular intellectual and cultural movement in Western Europe in the eighteenth century; the 'concept' of the Enlightenment is explained in *Dialektik der Aufklärung* by analysing the behaviour and character of Odysseus in Homer's *Odyssey* who is presented as the prototype of Enlightenment rationality.[37] Rather 'Enlightenment' is an abstract and 'speculative' construct which is supposed to designate the underlying and defining real tendency of Western history; it takes its name from the eighteenth-century movement because thinkers in the eighteenth century formulated with particular clarity a certain set of conceptions and theories, which are characteristic of the West from Homer to Hitler. All of Western history can be seen as a single unitary process in which those conceptions come to be ever more clearly formulated and increasingly realized on an ever wider scale and in more and more uncompromising forms.

As it were, the 'Whig' theory of history is correct in that history is unitary – it does have a single tendency that leads up to the present as its culmination – but it is wrong to think that this is unmitigated progress in any sense that would merit unconditional approval.

What, then is this Enlightenment conception of reason and what is wrong with it? It has two aspects. On the one hand it encompasses a commitment to certain substantive ideals of autonomy, humanity, non-coercion, individual human happiness etc. On the other hand it is committed to the view that the accumulation and spread of knowledge will advance these ideals. Unfortunately the conception of 'knowledge' embedded in the Enlightenment project is very restricted, and to take so severely limited a conception of 'knowledge' to be the very defining feature of reason is to make a very significant mistake. What is wrong with the 'Enlightenment', then, is that it has a seriously inadequate conception of reason, and its conception of reason is inadequate because it identifies reason with the accumulation of a very narrowly defined kind of knowledge. This may seem to be a mere mistake in theory of knowledge, but Adorno and Horkheimer think it has monumental consequences.

The Enlightenment construes knowledge as having three interconnected properties: a) it takes genuine knowledge to be objectifying knowledge, i.e. to be based on making a clear and strict distinction between the human subject and whatever is the object of knowledge; b) it takes genuine knowledge to be 'identifying', i.e. knowledge is increased by finding general concepts under which individual instances can be subsumed; something is considered to have been identified (and thus to be 'known') if and when it has been brought under an appropriate general concept, and different instances of the same general concept can within limits be treated as if they were 'identical' (i.e. instances of a general concept can be substituted for any other under appropriate circumstances);[38] and finally c) it takes genuine knowledge to be inherently instrumental, able to change the world and give us control over it. For a variety of complex reasons Horkheimer and Adorno believe that 'instrumental reason' – the pursuit of greater and greater control over the world through the accumulation and implementation of 'knowledge' – has an inherent tendency to absolutise itself.[39] This undermines the Enlightenment project thoroughly. The ideals of the Enlightenment can't show themselves to be 'rational' if 'rationality' is *defined* as instrumental rationality, and the growth of scientific knowledge and associated instrumentally rational forms of industrial, commercial, and bureaucratic organization in fact undermine the actual ability of people in the modern world to attain individual happiness, self-determination, etc. In the final analysis, then, instrumental reason that is the cause of the discrepancy between paradise and Auschwitz.

If we accept for the sake of argument that world is evil, and that this evil has something to do with the dominance of instrumental reason in the modern world, a number of immediate consequences follow for art. First of all any form of art (or of religion or philosophy for that matter) that contributed to trying to 'reconcile' people to this world or that caused them to affirm it would be not just mistaken, but defective in the most fundamental way possible. Such a form of art would be, as it were, 'sinful'. Just as the Christian doctrine of original sin didn't designate just some individual moral failing some particular person had, but a basic corruption of the will that infected *any* natural form of human willing, to live in a modern society is to live in a state of sin. If Adorno were following Hegel very closely he would avoid moralizing this part of his theory, but perhaps under the influence of Schönberg, who had a tendency to conflate the aesthetic and the moral (and occasionally also the religious), Adorno doesn't always do this and one often gets the sense that he thinks that any attempt to foster reconciliation, although ultimately the result of the fallen and sinful state of our world as whole, is *also* at least a quasi-moral failing. Thus in a famous passage from his *Minima Moralia*[40] he claims that 'nowadays it is part of morality not to be at home with one-self'.[41] In a radically evil society the task of art must be to contribute to a negative theodicy, to make people more consciously unhappy and dissatisfied with their lives, and especially to make them as keenly aware as possible of the dangers of instrumental rationality and the discrepancy between their world as potential paradise and their world as actual catastrophe.

Against this background one can see why taking entertainment as even a possible appropriate goal for art in the modern world is just out of the question for Adorno. People shouldn't be entertained if that means being rendered content while losing sight of the evil of the world. People's unreflectively given desires in our society are part and parcel of the evil whole and the satisfaction of them is complicitous with the maintenance of an evil world.[42] Art in the modern world shouldn't be about 'satisfaction' at all, but about telling the critical truth about our society (that it is evil).[43]

Art then in the modern world must work against its own in-built tendency to be affirmative, a tendency that has been reinforced by virtually its whole history until the end of the nineteenth century, and it must try to turn against its own nature and be as negative and critical as possible.[44] One of the ways it can best do this is by extracting itself as much as possible from the network of instrumental rationality and 'usefulness'. That art is useless for all practical purposes is an advantage. This is why Adorno rejects the notion of a directly politically engaged art such as that propagated by Brecht.[45] Art can be critical in the right way only if it remains true to its vocation and history. The history of art is one of increasing emancipation from all extra-artistic purposes, and in the modern world cultivating this autonomy turns out also to be the most effective way to be radically negative. Art is critical and negative through its form.

The most radically negative kind of art would be one which through exclusively artistic means turned the most fundamental received laws of a certain kind of artistic activity upside down precisely by treating these received laws, principles, and rules of procedure with the highest seriousness and developing them consistently in a non-arbitrary way into their opposite. This is the significance, for Adorno, of Schönberg's progress from Romanticism to atonalism.[46] Romanticism was committed to some principles of musical expressivity and originality; it was also committed to the tonal system. Schönberg's development 'shows' that this is an inconsistent set of demands and by showing this, tacitly criticizes Romanticism (and also indirectly the society of which Romanticism is an expression): The tonal system had by the end of the century become so 'exhausted' that the expressivity and, in particular, the originality Romanticism demanded of music couldn't be attained by using tonal means. Taking the extreme chromaticism of late Romanticism 'further', as earlier Romantics had taken existing earlier forms of chromaticism 'further', eventually meant abandoning the tonal system altogether.

The sense in which Schönberg's music 'shows' the inconsistency of Romanticism (or criticizes bourgeois society) is not one that will reveal itself if one simply considers any particular work of his, fully on its own, in complete isolation from its historical context and studies just its immediately perceptible properties, or analyses its formal structure. To appreciate the critical force of Schönberg one has to know the musical tradition and its place in wider social history and hear his music as part of that history. For anyone who is liable to listen to Schönberg's music seriously, though, this does not require going outside 'the music itself' and bringing to bear some extraneous bits of learned lore, because in some sense the history of Western music is already in our ears, in their accumulated habits and expectations of hearing, and if it weren't, not only would we fail to see Schönberg's music as critical, we would fail to be able to make sense of it at all. To the extent to which we are knowledgeable about music it will be because we are a part of this tradition and have built up the appropriate habits and expectations, and so, to some extent, we will be able to react to Schönberg's criticism without needing to have it explained to us. In one sense early audiences may not have 'understood' Schönberg's music, but in another they understood it all too well. The shock, horror, and rage with which the music was received is comprehensible if one assumes that earlier audiences did realize in some sense that their whole society and form of life was being assaulted.

Still assault is not quite the same thing as internal criticism, and Adorno also thinks that art needs philosophic interpretation as its necessary complement to develop its critical impetus into full-blown truth-telling.[47] This isn't quite the same kind of claim as Hegel's view that art is in some sense supplanted by philosophy, if only because Adorno has a very different view of 'philosophy' from Hegel. For Hegel, art and philosophy were distinct domains and philosophical argumentation was not at all like the production of the sensible forms of art; for Adorno philosophy itself has an irreducible aesthetic dimension, which at least suggests that the aesthetic is not as firmly subordinated to the conceptual as in Hegel.

As for Hegel, for Adorno, art is a necessary failure[48] – it can't really pull off the trick of turning radically against itself and its own tendency to affirmation while continuing to exist, and it can't *effectively* negate its own evil society – but the analysis of the failure can be of cognitive significance.

To put Adorno's views in outline then, using the same schema I used for Hegel, (*vide supra*) Adorno holds that (contemporary) art is successful if

a) it makes us aware of our own deepest interests
b) and shows us that these interests cannot be realized within our society

c) thereby distancing us further from reconciliation with our society
d) and generating in us a kind of kind of resistant melancholy, a sad refusal to participate in society

One might easily accept the rest of the analysis and remain slightly dubious about (d). Why should 'melancholy' be the appropriate affect rather than one of the affects that usually accompanies social activism (righteous indignation, solidarity, revolutionary enthusiasm)? Adorno's criticism of Western 'rationality', after all, was a criticism of it for being too instrumental, too concerned with being an effective guide to action. If one adds to this general theoretical suspicion of (instrumentally effective) action, Adorno's belief that society was a closed, all-encompassing 'totality' wielding overwhelming power over the individual, and almost infinitely capable of turning to its own (evil) purposes *any* form of action directed against it, it becomes easy to see that withdrawal into melancholy seems the only appropriate response. Adorno's pithy claim in *Minima Moralia*:[49] 'Es gibt kein richtiges Leben im falschen', which means roughly both: a) 'there is no real *living* in a false (form of) life' and b) 'there is no way to live *correctly* (as an individual) in a form of life that is itself false (as a whole)' can be seen as the *non plus ultra* of sophisticated reflection, but also as an excuse for doing nothing. Adorno had a genius for finding general reasons for doing what he wanted to do and for not doing things he wanted to avoid, although sometimes even he seemed to be scraping the bottom of the barrel of his theoretical imagination, as when at one point in the 1960s he claimed that he couldn't take part in a political demonstration because he was too fat (*'Das ist nichts für ältere Herren mit Embonpoint'*).

To the end of his life Adorno continued to argue that his position was not one of 'resignation', because he retained his grasp on the happiness (*Glück*) given by (non-instrumental) knowing, such as the 'cognition' provided by art and philosophic commentary, even though *what* he came to know was nothing but universal unhappiness (*Unglück*).[50] Although he doesn't mention it, it is also the case that he never allowed general theoretical considerations to interfere with his full enjoyment of the delights of the kind of life to which his inherited wealth gave him access. Lukács speaks of Adorno as inhabiting *Grand Hotel 'Abgrund'* where the *frisson* caused by the view down into the abyss of modern capitalist society was a picant addition to the general high level of luxurious comfort provided.[51] Adorno would have thought this remark very unfair, perhaps an expression of the envy petty-bourgeois intellectuals often direct at those who are more fortunate.[52] It is hard to believe this can be true of Lukács who, after all, came from a background at least as wealthy and privileged as Adorno's. Still perhaps Adorno is partly right about this. Even if he is, though, that may be no defense, since, to paraphrase another one of Adorno's *mots* from *Minima Moralia*, 'The splinter in my own eye may be the best magnifying glass'.[53] Also the main point of this line of criticism may not be that Adorno lived a life of comfort, but that he did so while criticizing the capitalist society that was the source and framework for his wealth, avoiding any action that would have been at all incovenient to himself, justifying his exclusive concern with his writing by reference to the purported impossibility of effective political action in the modern world, and claiming that in failing to become politically engaged he had not 'resigned'. Perhaps there really wasn't anything he could have done, but to many his position considered as a whole may seem too dialectical by half. The fact that Kant ran his life by rules, some of which seem to us fantastic, such as 'Never accept an offer of a coach ride (because it may make you late for an appointment)' or 'Never smoke more than *one* pipe of tobacco a day (but get a pipe big enough to last all day)' is not taken by most people as an argument against the doctrine of the categorical imperative. This is because we accept a distinction between arguments in philosophy as a moderately technical subject and the details of philosophers' everyday attitudes. Adorno, however, was committed to micrological analysis, to the study of the detail which illuminates the whole, and he was disinclined to draw a sharp distinction between technical philosophy and the general way in which one conducts one's life. Any evaluation of Adorno's philosophizing that tried to be true to the spirit of the approach he himself used in studying other philosophical positions would have to come to terms with Adorno's own extreme narcissism and the self-serving nature of his melancholy.

Nietzsche spent most of productive life trying to escape the pessimism he felt was the almost inevitable consequence a sensitive spirit in the late nineteenth century would draw from the collapse of Christianity. During his short philosophical career he changed his views about theodicy and art very considerably. I will first say something about the early position (outlined in his first book *Geburt der Tragödie*), then I will close with a few brief remarks about his later change of heart.

Originally Nietzsche thought that only what I have called above a 'false theodicy' is possible for us and that such a theodicy to be effective would have to be a form of art and not anything discursive. In a memorable phrase he asserts that the world and human life can be justified 'only as an aesthetic phenomenon'.[54] Although all artistic genres are aimed at giving a theodicy, the most effective is provided by tragedy, and so in what follows I will concentrate on tragedy.[55]

Nietzsche starts from two sets of assumptions taken over from Schopenhauer. The first is a series of metaphysical views. The everyday world we see around us, Schopenhauer claims, a world of individuated objects in space and time, held together through relations of causality, is an insubstantial appearance, the reality of which is a metaphysical entity which is not subject to any of our normal cognitive categories – it isn't spatial or temporal, and it isn't causally connected to anything in our world – and which Schopenhauer calls 'the Will'. Our world is then the way this Will and its action appears to us. The second assumption is Schopenhauer's pessimism: A careful reflection on human experience will show, as Nietzsche was later to put it, that 'life is worthless'.[56] There is an inherent lack of fit between essential human desires and the essential nature of human willing, on the one hand, and the possibilities the world offers of satisfying those desires, on the other. As a result, we humans are doomed to an unhappy life which careens back and forth erratically between frustration (when particular desires we have are not satisfied) and boredom (when particular desires we have had are satisfied).[57]

Nietzsche uses an image derived from Herakleitos to express the basic metaphysics which *Geburt der Tragödie* presupposes.[58] The reality behind appearances (Schopenhauer's 'Will') is like a wanton child playing on a beach. The Child draws figures in the sand and then wipes them out, taking equal pleasure in both activities (i.e. both in the creation of the individuated figures and in their destruction). Our world of appearances is the succession of momentary figures in the sand. Every empirical human being is no more than one such figure. This play follows no rational or moral rules; the Child is merely gratifying its aesthetic predilections. If the play has a structure at all it can only be a structure of aesthetic necessity.

Since the Child and its activity is (in some metaphysical sense) the reality of which I (along with all other human individuals) am a mere appearance, it shouldn't be out of the question for me to be able to see the world as it does, and even to share not just the Child's viewpoint, but the pleasure it takes in its activity. Art (especially tragic art) through the production of a seductive world of *Schein* allows us for a moment to do this.

The *Schein* tragedy produces is a complex phenomenon. The actor up on stage is not really a man who has just blinded himself with his recently deceased wife-mother's brooch, but just *seems* to be. That it is Oedipus on stage is a *Schein*. The audience in one sense knows this – anyone who thought the man on stage *really had* blinded himself would have failed to understand the artistic *Schein* that was being presented – but in another sense it lets itself be taken in by the illusory appearance to the extent at any rate of being moved emotionally by what it sees and hears (as if it were real). The fate of the tragic hero – suffering the collapse of an apparently well founded identity and the dissolution of individuality in death presented in a way that makes them seem necessary and inevitable – is really the fate of each of us. It is the final metaphysical truth about the world and human life. However, it is presented to us in tragedy *as if* it were something happening to someone else – to Oedipus, *not* to each of us – and that isn't exactly correct.

From the Child's point of view its own activity (and thus the resultant play of individuated forms in the world of mere appearance) is pleasurable and self-justifying, and everything in the world, all of life, will seem 'in order' – how could it not, given that the world as a whole is nothing but the result of the Child's following out its own predilections?

The reason discursive or conceptual thought will not work as a theodicy is that if one *reasons* correctly about the world, one will come to Schopenhauer's conclusion. The justificatory effect of art depends on enabling me to share the self-validating pleasure of the Child. Since the Child is me, is the reality of which I am a mere appearance, its pleasure is in some sense (potentially) mine, and art makes that potentiality actual. On the other hand, the Child is also not-me; the identification art encourages is also in some sense an illusion. I as an empirical person belong to a world of individuated objects, and am distinct from other persons; the Child is beyond the principle of individuation. What will satisfy the aesthetic sense of the Child – the random generation and destruction of individuated form – may not and in fact pretty certainly will not really be compatible with *my* deepest interests (as an individual), and the same will hold true of every other human individual. What looks just fine from the point of view of the Child – Raymond

dying painfully in a highly interesting and dramatic way –
won't be nearly so satisfactory to me as the empirical person I
am. The function of art is to give me a proper glimpse of *one* side
of the relation between the Child and me – the side of our
'identity', while at the same time hiding the other side from
me, *deceiving me* about the non-identity that exists between
myself and the Child, and the possible implications that has for
my ability to see my life as worthwhile. The *Schein* that constitutes art isn't a straightforward lie, because people who experience art in the right way don't take it to be the propounding of
some literal truth, but it is a deceptive appearance, which both
directs attention away from an important truth and actively
hides it from us. The particular combination of revelation of the
truth plus deception is characteristic of what art can do, but it is
not available to discursive forms of thought. To experience art
means to allow oneself to be deceived, but to be able to do that
does result in a genuine pleasure that is self-validating and
which can 'seduce' one to continue living.

To map this onto the scheme I have used before, then, for
Nietzsche art is successful if:

a) it effectively mystifies us about our own deepest interests
   by causing us to confuse them with those of the Child
b) it thus also mystifies us about the possibility of satisfying
   those interests
c) it overwhelms our potential cognitive recognition that
   life is not worth living for us by shedding a transfiguring
   glow over life as a whole and 'justifying' it to us
d) it thereby seduces us to continue to live.

This early position, then, combines cognitive pessimism with
an aesthetic theodicy in a very striking way, but one that depends crucially on the highly speculative construction Nietzsche in his later Preface to the second edition of *GT* calls with
only mildly disguised contempt the *'Artisten-Metaphysik'*, the

story of the divine Child who is the reality behind the world of appearances.

The later Nietzsche moves away from this position in two directions. First the whole task of theodicy presupposes that there could be such a thing as the objective constitution of the world, the way the world was in itself, and that this constitution of the world (or our correct cognition of it) could in some sense *require* us (or at least require us on pain of 'irrationality') to make a certain kind of value judgment about the world as a whole ('It is good') and adopt some affective attitude toward the world and our lives (for instance, an attitude of affirmation). Nietzsche, however, comes to think that this whole idea of the world requiring that we make a certain value judgment about it or adopt an attitude toward it, doesn't make sense.[59] Optimism and pessimism, if these are intended to designate 'justified' attitudes, i.e. attitudes grounded on *knowledge* of the way the world is, fall by the wayside, too, as does the whole project of giving a theodicy. The second strand in Nietzsche's later work is an attempt to extract possible ways of being affirmative from the apparatus of justification, optimism/pessimism, and theodicy.

Rejecting the basic framework of philosophical theodicy needn't mean giving up on theodicy as a naturalistic project – any of us who have survived to become more or less functional adults have done so in part because as infants we lived in a 'good enough' world, and so any survivors form a possible audience for a true naturalistic theodicy: For them, at any rate, the world *was* sufficiently rational and good, and with sufficient empirical knowledge one could tell a true story about how their empirical world provided an environment which allowed them to become the functional agents capable of affirmation and self-affirmation they have become.[60] Nor need the rejection of the traditional philosophical project of theodicy mean abandoning discussion of art in the context of the generation, cognition, and satisfaction of human interests. We might still be able to make some distinction between deeper and more superficial human interests. It isn't even out of the question that we might still be able to make some distinction between real or true and merely apparent or false interests. We might still be able to speak of ways in which particular art-works or genres contributed to making us aware of or deluding us about our pre-existing interests, or ways in which they helped to bring new human interests into being; one such 'new' human interest might be in a way of life in which specific (perhaps novel) forms of artistic activity could be cultivated. Finally we might still be able to speak sensibly about ways in which art could perhaps satisfy (or fail to satisfy) either pre-existing interests or interests it creates itself. Failure might be as important as or even more important than success; Hegel and Adorno might well be right about that. It isn't, after all, self-evident that a form of art or a work of art will itself necessarily satisfy the interests it generates. One might rather think that it was a sign of an especially significant work that it *didn't* do this, that it was (in part) a promise only something *else*, another work of art or another kind of everyday life, could keep. This might be one of the ways in which art could be part of the motor of a certain kind of historical development. For the later Nietzsche the question in any case would be what role art could play in a life that was affirmative, but not optimistic.

NOTES

1 *Metaphysics*, 982b11ff.
2 Thus Feuerbach (in *das Wesen des Christentums*) explained the origin of religion as a reaction to experience of our own inadequacy, frustration, or powerlessness. To compensate for experienced failure we fantasize an entity who has in abundance the powers we have just been shown to lack.
3 Obviously how far we 'can' really change some of these expectations is unclear.

4 Hegel criticizes Leibniz' attempt to give a theodicy on the grounds that Leibniz incorrectly assumes that the standards used in such a theodicy are antecedently given and fixed. Cf. *Vorlesungen über die Geschichte der Philosophie* (cited according to G.W.F Hegel, *Werke in zwanzig Bänden,* Suhrkamp, Frankfurt, 1970 [hereinafter abbreviated *HW*] by volume and page): *HW* 20.247ff.

5 This isn't exactly correct because the basic entities for Hegel are not 'humans' but forms of *Geist.* All humans are, for Hegel, (essentially) *Geist* but *Geist* is a category that is in principle more encompassing than 'human' is. There are, for instance, not just finite, but also 'infinite' *Geister* for Hegel, e.g. God. To put the matter as I have here covers over the distinction between Hegel on the one hand and the naturalization of the Hegelian position in Feuerbach and the early Marx on the other, but this distinction is not of direct relevance for the points I wish to make here.

6 *HW* 13.50ff; cf. also *HW* 7.11–28

7 There is another part of the story which tells how this 'modern' world of abstract institutions confronting highly individualized persons comes into being historically. 'Originally' humans lived in a state of what Hegel calls 'unmediated unity' with nature and the surrounding world.

8 For Hegel virtually everything is a question of degree. Generally a person isn't 'free' or 'unfree' but free to some extent etc.

9 Cf. Michael Hardimon, *Hegel's Social Philosophy: The Project of Reconciliation* (CUP, 1994) and Allen Wood, *Hegel's Ethical Theory* (CUP, 1990). An aspect of Hegel's theory that will play no role in my discussion is his view that to attain reconciliation means at the same time to have become free.

10 *HW* 12.28.

11 This idea that a society might have forms of art, religion, and philosophy which falsely exhibited the society as rational and good is one of the origins of the traditional Marxist concept of 'ideology'.

12 At the end of the lectures on the philosophy of history Hegel refers to philosophy, presumably his own philosophy, as a *'wahrhafte Theodizee'* (*HW* 20.454f). *'Wahrhaft'* ('genuine' i.e. 'true' in the sense in which someone can be called a 'true' friend) doesn't, of course, in general mean *'wahr'* ('true' in a cognitive sense). Also Hegel is here in the first instance contrasting philosophy with religion, which, as we will see, keeps trying but failing to be a theodicy. Still for Hegel, given what a theodicy is and aspires to be,

a 'genuine' one can only be one that is 'true' (in the cognitive sense).

13 Hegel's account of why people don't understand that they ought to be reconciled to their world seems to be that there is in general a kind of historical lag in human awareness of history. People now fail to understand the present because they are still in the grip of various 'abstractions'. (Cf. *HW* 7.26.)

14 Note that Lukács at least in some of his moods (e.g. in *Geschichte und Klassenbewußtsein* [Luchterhand 1968], especially the section III *'Die Antinomien des bürgerlichen Denkens'* in the long essay *'Verdinglichung und das Bewußtsein des Proletariats'*) argues in a not dissimilar way in favour of acknowledging a certain cognitive superiority of Kant over Hegel. Since, on Lukács's Marxist view, both lived in a capitalist society which was very much not 'in order' it was impossible for them to provide a true theodicy. The question was, then, how they would deal with the necessary failure of their basic philosophic project. Kant, as became a sturdy devotee of the categorical imperative, took the path of honesty even at the price of incoherence. The insoluble difficulties of his views about the relation of the empirical and the transcendental, the phenomenal and the noumenal are the reflection of his success in *correctly* reflecting antinomies that existed in his society. On the other hand, Hegel's metaphysical appeals to *'Vernunft'* as a higher cognitive power capable of seeing in synthetic unity what *'Verstand'* has divided (so as to allow us to be reconciled with an inherently antinomic social reality) was a comforting illusion about early nineteenth-century European society (although, on the other hand, it also represented the development of a method which would allow later thinkers, especially Marxists, to understand how one could get beyond those antinomies by changing society).

15 Cf. *supra,* discussion of notion of an 'absolute' interest.

16 Again with the proviso that for Hegel himself the fact that these interests develop over time is no argument against the possibility of ordering them retrospectively into a unitary rational scheme. I must admit that this section of my account of Hegel is perhaps on especially weak ground given the extreme difficulty in understanding the relation between the philosophical account of the world he thinks he is able to give 'from the absolute standpoint' and his recognition of the historical nature of all the particular phenomena he treats.

17 This section is obviously a rather free development of some Hegelian themes rather than a strict interpretation of his views. He doesn't, as I have mentioned in the main text, strictly distinguish between needs and interests. In fact in this example one could just as easily speak of a post-Christian 'need' for satisfaction of the aspiration to individual happiness as of an 'interest in' individual happiness and welfare. Nor does Hegel use an example like this one, which I have invented. The closest he comes is his discussion of seventeenth-century Dutch painting (*HW* 13.222ff). The representation of domestic scenes, he claims, doesn't condemn this kind of painting to insignificance, because at that period the domestic was part of the content of people's deepest interests.

18 Cf. *HW* 13.100; 115ff, *HW 14.237* etc.

19 Cf. *HW* 13.82 etc.

20 Cf. *HW* 3.56–67; 5.92ff.

21 *HW* 13.23.

22 *HW* 7.27.

23 *HW* 10.367.

24 *HW* 10.367.

25 *HW* 10.367.

26 *HW* 10.366f; 13.116 etc.

27 *HW* 13.151.

28 *HW* 13.64–82.

29 Hegel distinguishes what he calls 'objective spirit' (essentially forms of objectified will, social institutions etc., cf. *HW* 10.300–305) from 'absolute spirit' (ways in which actually existing spirit comes to know itself, cf. *HW* 10.366f). The sphere of objective spirit (i.e. morality and politics) is not free-standing or self-justifying for Hegel, but needs a guarantee (or confirmation) from absolute spirit (cf. *HW* 7.417;10.355ff;13.137ff).

30 *HW* 13.140ff.

31 *HW* 13.142.

32 *HW* 13.25f; 140ff.

33 For an older but still useful discussion, cf. Rudolf Haym, *Die Romantische Schule* (Olms, Hildesheim,1961, photomechanical reproduction of first edition, Berlin, 1890), pp. 250ff.

34 At a generous estimate half a dozen of the roughly 1000 pages of Hegel's aesthetics are devoted to a discussion of the novel.

35 Adorno, *Ästhetische Theorie* (Suhrkamp, Frankfurt/M,1970 [hereinafter abbreviated *ÄT*]) pp. 65ff *et passim*.

36 *ÄT* 55f.

37 M. Horkheimer and T. W. Adorno, *Dialektik der Aufklärung* (Fischer, Frankfurt, 1969), pp. 50ff.

38 Obviously it is crucial here to specify what 'appropriate circumstances' are. This second purported property is the one that is most important for Adorno and the one to the analysis of which he devotes most of his attention. A large part of the work of his which resembles most closely a normal philosophical treatise, *Negative Dialektik* (Suhrkamp, 1966; esp. pp. 140–161), is an investigation of the issues surrounding what he calls 'identity-thinking'.

39 Horkheimer and Adorno, *Dialektik der Aufklärung*, p.12.

40 Suhrkamp (Frankfurt, 1951), §18.

41 Adorno's inversion of the Hegelian motif in this passage is characteristic. It is also characteristic that in the section from which this snippet is taken Adorno is discussing domestic arrangements (e.g. whether beds should be close to the floor or not). If society really is an all-encompassing 'totality' which informs even the smallest and seemingly most unimportant details of private life, then microscopic analysis of such details could in principle yield very significant insights. Hegel, in contrast, was much more inclined to consign such details to the category of 'the particular', to claim that they were merely contingent, and of no inherent philosophical interest, once one had seen in general that they were contingent, and pass over them in silence. Adorno seems to have derived this interest in micrological analysis from Walter Benjamin. On this general topic cf. S. Buck-Morss, *The Origin of Negative Dialectics* (Free Press, New York, 1977).

42 *ÄT*, 26.

43 Cf. *Impromptus* (Suhrkamp, 1968), pp. 20f. where Adorno says he 'doubts' that music exists 'for the sake of people'. This presumably that it needn't (or even shouldn't) be directed at pleasing them, i.e. at satisfying their existing taste. He also says he doubts that music can have any moral effect. Its vocation is just to tell the truth and produce 'correct consciousness' in those who listen to it.

44 *ÄT* 10,239f.

45 Adorno's most thematic discussion of these issues is contained in two essays, *'Erpreßte Versöhnung'* and *'Engagement'* (respectively in volumes II and III of his *Noten zur Literatur* [Suhrkamp, 1961 and 1965]).

46 Cf. T.W. Adorno, *Gesammelte Schriften* (Suhrkamp, 1978), vol. 16, pp. 68ff, 606ff; (Suhrkamp, 1984), vol. 18, pp. 363ff, 385ff.

47 *ÄT* 141f, 193ff.

48 *ÄT* 87.
49 *Minima Moralia* (Suhrkamp, Frankfurt/M,1951), §18.
50 Adorno, *'Resignation'* (written 1969), in *Kritik: Kleine Schriften zur Gesellschaft* (Suhrkamp, Frankfurt, 1971), pp. 145ff.
51 *'Vorwort'* to the second edition of *Theorie des Romans* (Luchterhand, 1962).
52 *Minima Moralia,* §1.
53 *Minima Moralia,* §29.
54 As Nietzsche himself points out in the preface to the second edition of *GT* (*'Versuch einer Selbstkritik'*, §5), slight variants of this phrase occur more than once in *GT.*
55 I discuss the issues raised in the following paragraphs in somewhat greater detail in my Introduction to the new edition of *GT* (translated by R. Speirs) to be published in the *Cambridge Texts in the History of Philosophy* series.
56 *'Das Leben . . . taugt nichts',* GD *'Das Problem des Sokrates',* §1.
57 For an especially good discussion of this cf. Julian Young *Willing and Unwilling: A Study in the Philosophy of Arthur Schopenhauer* (Nijhoff 1987), esp. chapter X.
58 *GT* §24, derived from Herakleitos' fragment 52: '. . . αἰὼν παῖς ἐστι παίζων πεσσεύων' (citing from Diels-Kranz *Fragmente der Vorsokratiker* [Weidman, Zürich, 1996]). I take it that *GM* II.16 contains a reference to the same fragment.
59 *GD, 'Das Problem des Sokrates',* §2,
60 Cf. Jonathan Lear, *Love and its Place in Nature* (Farrar, Straus & Giroux, New York, 1990).

# 5

## ADORNO AND BERG

W HEN Berg was in Frankfurt for the premiere of the *Three Fragments from 'Wozzeck'* in 1924 he was introduced to a twenty-one-year-old student named Theodor Wiesengrund. Wiesengrund was about to submit a doctoral dissertation in philosophy on the then fashionable topic of Husserlian phenomenology, but he also had some training as a musician and had published a number of journalistic pieces on contemporary music. Later, Wiesengrund would claim that at the time he saw in Berg a representative of the 'true new music' – 'at the same time Schönberg and Mahler'.[1] He proposed to move to Vienna to study composition with Berg as soon as the formalities for the granting of his doctoral degree were completed. Berg agreed to take him as a student.

Wiesengrund was the only son of a wealthy Jewish wine merchant, Oskar Wiesengrund, and of Maria Calvelli-Adorno, a French singer. He was a highly intelligent, deeply cultured and aesthetically sensitive young man, but had in some ways a not very attractive character. Schönberg found his oily, self-important manner, arrogance and beady-eyed stare repulsive,[2] and certainly Wiesengrund's writings give the impression of being the work of a more than usually self-absorbed person. Despite this, Berg seems to have had a genuine affection for him and a high opinion of his compositions, although no interest at all in his philosophical speculations.[3]

For a time Wiesengrund composed while also pursuing a university career in philosophy, but during the 1930s he gradually gave up composition altogether,[4] although he continued to write about music until his death in 1969. The Nazis deprived him of his university post in 1933, but he didn't believe Hitler would last long in power[5] and also, according to one of his friends, 'couldn't believe that anything could happen to *him*, the son of Oskar Wiesengrund,'[6] so he temporised. In 1937, just after Berg's death, a number of analyses of Berg's work by Wiesengrund appeared in the volume edited by Willi Reich;[7] these had a certain influence on early interpretations of Berg. Finally in 1938 Wiesengrund emigrated to New York. At about the same time he began to use his mother's maiden name, Adorno, as his surname.[8]

In the early 1940s Adorno (as he now was) wrote the work that was to be his major contribution to thinking about music, *Philosophie der neuen Musik*.[9] He was working on the manuscript at just the time when his neighbour in the German exile community in California, Thomas Mann, was beginning to write his fictional life of the German composer 'Adrian Leverkühn' which eventually appeared as the novel *Doktor Faustus* (1947). Mann wanted to include some detailed descriptions of imaginary compositions by 'Leverkühn' in the novel and Adorno's presence was a godsend. In 1943 Adorno gave Mann a copy (in manuscript) of the theoretically most interesting part of *Philosophie der neuen Musik*, the chapter on Schönberg, and he served in general as musical advisor to Mann.[10] Adorno was later to point to some similarities between Berg and Leverkühn, but these seem actually to be relatively superficial.[11] Thomas Mann himself always claimed that Leverkühn was a fictional creation with composite traits derived from a variety of sources. It is certainly hard to see much of the Austrian-Catholic Berg, who was so given to the enjoyment of good food and drink (and whose comment on German cuisine was: 'the Germans only ever eat muck')[12] in the cold ascetic German-Protestant Leverkühn.[13]

After the war Adorno returned to Frankfurt and was active in the reconstruction of musical life there. He tried to enlist

Thomas Mann's help in preventing the reopening of Bay-reuth[14] and was a regular feature of the Darmstadt scene. He continued to publish copiously on music – in 1968, the year before his death, he published a monograph on Berg which incorporated the material he had originally written for the 1937 Reich volume – but his work never again attained the energy, imaginativeness and acuity it had had in the 1940s.[15]

ART AND AFFIRMATION

Adorno took a basically Hegelian approach to art characterised by three theses:[16]

- the central aesthetic category is not 'beauty' (for instance), but 'truth'
- (aesthetic) 'truth' stands in a close inherent relation to history
- the history of music should be understood as a dialectic between Subject (in this case the 'musical' or 'compositional' subject, a composer with characteristic powers and sensibilities) and Object (in this case what Adorno calls 'the musical material').

There is, Adorno assumes, a single unilinear historical path of development of music. At any point in time a composer confronts a pre-given musical language, and a set of musical forms and aesthetic demands – this is the 'material' – and tries to structure this 'material' into a coherent work of art, using existing compositional techniques, or more or less radical modifications of such techniques. It is essential to keep firmly in mind that what Adorno calls 'the material' is not the physical (e.g. the acoustic) basis of music, not notes considered as natural phenomena; rather 'the material', what the composer finds already there and must deal with in order to produce a work, is a historically and culturally formed body of expectations, demands, expressive features, etc. Such 'material' is itself at any given time the *result* of previous compositional activity, and highly innovative compositional activity *now* will, as it were, become absorbed in and thus change the 'material' the next generation of composers will confront.

A further feature of Adorno's account is his claim that up to now (or at any rate up to Adorno's death in 1969) no fully satisfactory, stable state of compositional practice has been attained. The demands and expectations embodied in the musical material are not at any time fully consistent, and attempts by the 'musical subject' to use existing (or newly invented) techniques to introduce coherence into works shaped from that material will never be fully successful. One can look at the same historical process in two complementary ways: depending on which perspective one adopts, that of the subject (the composer) or that of the object (the musical material), one can see the whole process as one in which active agents (composers) imaginatively invent new forms and techniques, thereby continually transforming the 'material' of music; or one can see the process as one in which the material is itself making demands, setting puzzles to which composers respond as best they can, finding more or less satisfactory solutions.

There is always a state-of-the-art of music, a set of techniques of composing, aesthetic canons of correctness and expressivity; there is also a set of demands the material (at that particular time) makes. Serious music is state-of-the-art music which addresses the demands of the musical material. Aesthetically successful music advances the state-of-the-art; it is innovative and progressive. This innovation or originality, however, is historically located in two ways. First, no matter how radically 'new' a given procedure or form is, it will always turn out to be a modification of existing techniques; second, for an innovation to be more than an idiosyncrasy or theoretical trifle, it must be used to deal with historically specific problems posed by the musical material. What is genuinely 'new' thus has high positive value, but it is this historical element in 'the new' that distinguishes Adorno's conception from an apparently very similar one found in French modernism. Baudelaire's *voyageurs* who sail under their captain Death 'pour trouver du *nouveau*' are motivated by ennui, horror and perhaps disgust, or by the sheer desire for novelty for its own sake.[17] Ever since the Epicureans at least, it has been pointed out, however, that Death is the radical Other of life, not a modified form of living; thus whatever new thing might exist 'au fond du gouffre' it is not something the *voyageurs* intend to bring back to improve existing techniques either of living or of making music.[18] Ennui is not the most obvious motivation of a composer trying to respond to the demands of the musical material, and indeed it is hard to imagine any of Baudelaire's *voyageurs* exhibiting the loving, meticulous devotion to tradition required to write a book like Schönberg's *Harmonielehre* – although writing such a book is a perfectly reasonable thing to do for a composer who is trying to learn how to respond to the historically given demands of the musical 'material'.

The idea that in successful aesthetic activity there is a kind of reconciliation of 'freedom' and 'necessity' – that the highest exercise of spontaneous freedom is precisely to find the 'necessary' solution to a problem – is one that goes back to the end of the eighteenth century and finds full and explicit expression in Schelling's *System des transzendentalen Idealismus* (1800). I merely note at this point that the notion of 'necessity' involved here is problematic and seems to presuppose some very strong claims about the 'demands' the 'material' makes. To speak of successful composition as reconciling freedom and necessity would seem to require that the 'demands' of the material have great specificity and that there is a unique 'correct', or at least uniquely 'best' way to satisfy them.[19]

Up to this point, Adorno's account in *Philosophie der neuen Musik* follows a generalised Hegelian position rather closely.

Now he adds two novel twists. First of all he identifies 'progressive' music in the historical–aesthetic sense – music that embodies new techniques to solve the problems posed by the material – with music that is 'progressive' in a political sense. Correspondingly, music that does not advance the state-of-the-art along the uniquely determined path required by the demands of the material is not just aesthetically unsatisfactory, but also politically reactionary. In *Philosophie der neuen Musik* Schönberg (and his school) function as the exemplary representatives of 'progressive', genuinely 'new' music and Stravinsky as the representative of reactionary 'neo-classicism'. No compromise between Schönberg and Stravinsky is possible, no intermediary position can be found.[20] To try to support this view Adorno has to engage in quite a lot of not very convincing dialectical manœuvres. Thus the second half of *Philosophie der neuen Musik* tries to argue that Stravinsky's music is 'psychotic', 'infantile', 'hebephrenic', 'depersonalised', 'alienated' and politically reactionary, despite the lack of evidence that Stravinsky himself held right-wing political views or was in any way supported or even especially warmly received in right-wing circles.[21] A continuing theme of Adorno's discussion of Berg will be his attempt to 'defend' him against the view that he represents a 'moderate' form of modern music, that is, occupies a kind of intermediate position the viability of which Adorno is committed to denying.

The second deviation from Hegelianism is connected with Adorno's doctrine of the 'dialectic of enlightenment'.[22] At a first approximation, the distinction between the members of the Second Viennese School and representatives of 'neo-classicism' seemed to be a division between sheep and goats, between the saved and the children of perdition, but on closer inspection the 'progress' represented by Schönberg and his students is not an unmixed blessing. The central tenet of the Enlightenment, according to Adorno, is that the human subject by gaining instrumental control over nature can escape from blind subjugation to 'fate' (and 'myth') and attain autonomy and happiness. For complex and not perhaps finally very clear philosophical reasons which Adorno expounds at great length in *Die Dialektik der Aufklärung*,[23] the process of enlightenment has an inherent tendency to turn against itself, so that the system of tools, social institutions, imperatives of rationality, etc., which was supposed to give us mastery of our fate, instead enslaves us. Effective long-term control of nature requires that we inhibit our spontaneous reactions to the world and adapt our mode of behaviour (and eventually even our mode of feeling) to the laws we discover in nature. In the long run such loss of spontaneity empties our subjectivity of content and can eventually deprive us of the very possibility of human happiness. Nature, mastered and objectified, has its revenge.

Adorno interprets Schönberg's development through atonality to the method of composing 'with twelve notes related only to each other' as an instance of the dialectic of enlightenment. The musical material of tonality has become a kind of (second) nature by the end of the nineteenth century. The breakthrough to atonality is a process in which the musical subject frees itself from the constraints of the material and establishes a kind of rational mastery over it. However, the absolute freedom of atonality leads by a 'necessary' progression to the even more rationally effective twelve-note method. In twelve-note music the 'material' (i.e. second 'nature') seems once again to be dictating to the subject after the brief fling of free atonality.[24]

> The subject dominates music through the rationality of the system, only in order to succumb to the rational system itself. . . .
> The new ordering of twelve-tone technique virtually extinguishes the subject.[25]

The 'musical subject' in Schönberg can thus become as 'depersonalised' as that which one finds in Stravinsky. So the two antipodes, Schönberg and Stravinsky, are not after all that far apart.[26] Rather, they are held together in a fellowship of necessary failure, because the unredeemed state of the world makes fully realised, adequate, satisfactory art impossible. The only form of even relative 'success' accessible to art is to indicate through its own very fragmentariness, inconsistency, its defects and sharp edges, the inherent inadequacy of the world we live in.[27] To do this would be for art to attain the truth to which it can aspire.

Adorno sometimes puts this point by saying that a traditional work of art is 'affirmative': it operates by means of a logic of tension/conflict and resolution and is successful when it observes the Leibnitzian principle of economy or parsimony[28] in developing and resolving the tension – making the greatest variety of forms out of the least material with the least 'effort' – and when in addition that *formal* resolution is also experienced as an affirmation of the fact that the world, despite appearances to the contrary, is basically in order, 'rational', and 'good'. 'Affirmative' art, Adorno claims, is now 'false' because our world is not fundamentally in order but radically evil. 'New' music must therefore satisfy the almost impossible demand of creating works of coherence which satisfy the highly developed aesthetic sensibilities of the best contemporary practitioners, while avoiding the use of any device or form that would allow one to experience or interpret the aesthetic properties of the work as an affirmation of the world as it is. Unfortunately art by its very nature is affirmative. The very fact that an internally coherent, aesthetically satisfying work has been produced tends to promote reconciliation with the world. If 'new' art *must* be non-affirmative, it must in some sense be trying not to be art at all, trying to undermine the very idea of the rounded, aesthetically satisfying art-work: 'Today the only works which really count are those which are no longer works at all'.[29] Thus art may now simply be impossible.

### BERG AND THE AVOIDANCE OF AFFIRMATION

This idea that genuinely 'new' (and thus 'true') art in the twentieth century must be non-affirmative is of great importance, so to get a clearer view of what is meant it might be useful to look at an example.

As is well known, after completing *Wozzeck*, Berg hesitated for a long time between two projects for a second opera. One was for an opera based on Hauptmann's *Und Pippa tanzt!*, the other for an opera to be based on two plays by Frank Wedekind about 'Lulu' (*Erdgeist* and *Die Büchse der Pandora*).[30] Some of Berg's friends thought *Und Pippa tanzt!* more promising,[31] and Adorno tried to take some credit for encouraging Berg to use the Lulu plays rather than Hauptmann's text.[32] Berg, however, initially ignored Adorno's advice and set to work on *Und Pippa tanzt!* Only when the financial negotiations for the rights to Hauptmann's play broke down did he turn instead to Wedekind.

*Und Pippa tanzt!* is a kind of *Zauberflöte* without the happy ending. The Tamino and Pamina figures (Michel and Pippa) fail their test. She dies; he is blinded and sent off to wander from Silesia to 'Venice' (i.e. through virtually the whole length of Habsburg Austria) to live by begging and playing his ocarina. The text presents a number of obvious opportunities for superficially striking musical effects. Apart from Michel's ocarina there is a scene in which Pippa runs her finger around the rim of a glass, the sound gradually getting louder and transforming itself into music.[33] Pippa and her father, Tagliazoni (who is lynched at the end of Act I for cheating at cards), speak in a mixture of German and Italian; the Monostatos figure ('Old Huhn') speaks in Silesian dialect and has a fine repertory of groans, shouts and other inarticulate noises; he kills Pippa by breaking a glass while she is dancing. It is true, as Adorno points out, that the play has some signal dramatic deficiencies: it is disjointed and uneven in tone and pace, and the plot rather loses momentum half way through. These need not, however, have been fatal to the work considered as a possible libretto. After all, a play could scarcely have *less* dramatic momentum than large parts of *Tristan* or a sillier and less integrated plot than *Zauberflöte,* and Berg would no doubt have introduced improvements when he produced the libretto. What would disqualify the play as 'new' art for Adorno lies deeper.

*Und Pippa tanzt!* begins in a world much like that of *Wozzeck,* a tavern in a small mountain village in which the only local industry, a glassworks, has closed. The tavern is full of unemployed and casual workers. Act I ends with a realistically presented disaster, the death of Tagliazoni and the abduction of Pippa by Old Huhn, but as the play progresses this real catastrophe is dissolved into a series of fairy-tale events culminating in a very traditional ending in which the blinded hero Michel, now off to a life of begging, is offered illusory consolation for his suffering: 'If people threaten to throw stones at you, tell them you are a prince . . . tell them about your water-palace.' It is just this kind of 'transfiguration' of suffering, 'tragic reconciliation' with fate, which Adorno believes to be characteristic of traditional 'affirmative' art and which he thinks 'new' art must reject on both aesthetic and political grounds.[34]

The ending of *Wozzeck* is quite emphatically not 'affirmative' in this sense. Perhaps it might have been just barely possible to take it in that way if the opera had ended with the orchestral interlude after Wozzeck's death (Act III scene 4): the (tonal) interlude might have been thought to suggest that a certain pharisaical kind of moral order had been established ('Poor man murders faithless wife and then drowns himself'). This way of taking it won't work, though, because Act III scene 5 shows us Wozzeck and Marie's young son. *He* isn't mystified into thinking real suffering has some deeper meaning or significance. He simply doesn't even yet realise what has happened, but we can be reasonably sure he will soon enough. It is quite wrong to suggest, as Fritz Heinrich Klein did in his review in *Musikblätter des Anbruch* in 1923, that 'the sight of the innocent orphaned child arouses a deep melancholy in the sympathetic soul and the hope that fate will be kinder to him than it has been to his parents'.[35] Berg points out in his lecture on *Wozzeck* that the opera ends with a *'perpetuum mobile* movement' and suggests that 'the opening bar of the opera could link up with [the] final bar and in so doing close the whole circle'.[36] The clear implication of this is that any hopes aroused in the 'sympathetic soul' are grossly illusory and that the child's future will be the same kind of cycle of confusion, pain, violence and despair we have just seen Wozzeck endure and exhibit.

There does seem to be a clear distinction between plays like *Und Pippa tanzt!* which are in some sense 'affirmative' and dramas like *Wozzeck* (or *Woyzeck* if we are speaking of the play)[37] which are not. Adorno, however, when he is at his most uncompromising, drawing out the implications of his own position with the greatest dialectical rigour, argues that even *Wozzeck* (the Berg opera) is in its own way 'affirmative'. It is, after all, still a coherent 'work' exhibiting aesthetic closure, and thus to that extent something that transfigures pain and leads to a resigned acceptance of it.[38] In the passage in which Adorno makes this argument (early in *Philosophie der neuen Musik*) he is contrasting *Wozzeck* (and *Lulu*), on the one hand, with Schönberg's *Erwartung and Die glückliche Hand* on the other. The implication seems to be that the latter really *are* non-affirmative non-works of art.

One might think that Adorno is simply confused here. It seems very odd to argue that *Erwartung* is not as much a *work* as *Wozzeck*. In addition, it is perfectly reasonable to present arguments against art in general: art won't cure real pain; perhaps it does foster the wrong attitudes in people. It isn't obvious, though, that such general arguments against the very existence of art can easily be transformed into internal aesthetic standards, ways of telling better art from worse art. True, art doesn't abolish the pain of the world, but that won't tell us anything about the relative merits of Schönberg and Stravinsky.

But to argue in this way against Adorno is to misunderstand his basic procedure (which is not, of course, to defend that basic procedure, but only to assert that criticism which wishes properly to engage Adorno would have to be differently couched). As Adorno repeatedly emphasises, he is engaged in 'dialectics' – in what he later came to call 'negative dialectics' – and such a dialectic is a corkscrew that is in principle *indefinitely* further extensible. What assertion one makes depends on where one is in the dialectical process. *Wozzeck* is non-affirmative (compared to *Und Pippa tanzt!*), but is still affirmative because still a work of art (relative to *Erwartung*), but *Erwartung* itself is still art and so committed to an affirmation which it itself tries to undermine. To adopt this position, however, would seem to mean accepting that art is impossible (because a work of art would have to be a work that is not a work), but great composers are precisely those who can make the impossible possible, who can square the circle: 'every piece of Berg's was extracted by subterfuge from its own impossibility'.[39] For Adorno, the dialectical process can have no natural stopping place. This is a good thing too, because such a dialectic is the expression of free human subjectivity. The end of the dialectic would be a kind of mental (and emotional) death.

As Adorno also points out,[40] Wedekind's second play about Lulu (*Die Büchse der Pandora*) does *not* end with the Countess Geschwitz's 'Liebestod' but rather with her calling out 'O, verflucht' ('Oh damn!'). Friedrich Cerha holds that it was Berg's final intention that Geschwitz *not* sing (or speak) the word 'verflucht', so his edition of the score very oddly gives her a final C♮ and B♭ after '. . . in Ewigkeit', but no text to sing to these two notes.[41] I must say that I agree with what I take to be the implications of Adorno's account in *Philosophie der neuen Musik:* to delete the final 'verflucht' spoils the whole ending, and if Berg did not intend to use this last bit of Wedekind's text he made a serious mistake. Geschwitz is *not* going to be joined with Lulu 'in Ewigkeit'; she is a frustrated woman whom we have seen to be capable of great and selfless love, but who is now dying miserably in a garret in London. Her final curse will tend to keep the audience's collective mind appropriately focused on that fact.

Of Berg's later works, the *Lyric Suite* is relatively easy to fit into this scheme of an essentially non-affirmative music: the Largo desolato which ends the piece is about as despairing and lacking in any form of transfiguration, metaphysical hope or consolation as one could imagine. The piece even has a structural feature which makes it less affirmative than *Wozzeck*, namely the ending in which the three other instruments successively drop away leaving only the viola, which is to repeat the same sequence of D♭–F, *diminuendo* and *morendo* 'until it is extinguished completely', but the point at which the violist is to stop is not unequivocally indicated. Berg's instructions are 're-peat the final third D♭–F *possibly* once or twice'. This 'open' ending can be seen as a way of dissolving the aesthetic closure characteristic of a 'work of art' from within.[42] This effect is perhaps even more striking on the page than it is when simply listening to the piece, because when the violinists and the cellist stop playing they are not given written-out rests in full score: instead, their very staves disappear.

Adorno connects this avoidance of metaphysical affirmation with a technical feature of Berg's music. In it, Adorno claims, one does not generally find fully-formed distinct themes, each with its own clear identity, which can be stated in full at the beginning, then developed and transformed and finally reinstated in triumph. Rather, each of Berg's works is like an infusorium in which tiny units of structure are constantly transforming themselves into other microscopic structures.[43] The units involved are so small and the process of transformation is so continuous that one never gets the sense of a determinate point at which one 'theme' begins and another ends, or of what is the 'original' form of a 'theme' and what a modification. To the extent to which there *are* many 'themes', Berg allows them to arise through a series of gradual, almost imperceptible transitions. The moment any 'theme' with a determinate structure *does* succeed in getting itself stated, Berg immediately begins gradually to decompose it back into the minimal elements from which it arose. So the basic structure of Berg's music is not 'tension/resolution' but 'construction/deconstruction' ('Aufbau/Abbau'), or one of asserting and taking back what was asserted. This 'taking back' is the opposite of traditional forms of musical affirmation.[44]

One might be tempted to see this Bergian gesture of 'taking back' as another point of similarity to Mann's 'Adrian Leverkühn', who at the end of the novel wants to write a work that 'takes back' the affirmation of life found at the end of the last movement of Beethoven's Ninth Symphony. Adorno himself might seem to foster this identification by referring at one point to Berg's 'dynamic nihilism'.[45] 'Dynamic nihilism' is perhaps an appropriate way to characterise the attitude of Leverkühn and of his political analogues, the Nazis, but, as Adorno writes in other places,[46] Berg's own attitude was not one of active, engaged nihilism, but of passive, melancholy resignation: sad contemplation of the transitoriness and frailty of a world in which all structures crumble under their own weight, rather than a desire to kick down what is already about to fall.[47]

If one asks, then, in what the 'truth' of Berg's music consists (according to Adorno), an important part of the answer is Berg's refusal of 'affirmation'. The basic sadness of his music shows that he is not 'reconciled'; his 'resignation' is that of a person who makes utopian demands on life and sees them eternally unsatisfied, but does not give them up.[48]

## HISTORICITY

The other component of Berg's 'truth' is his acceptance of historicity. Berg does *not* take the path down which later serialism would go in the direction of 'bad ahistoricity', but rather continues to attempt to combine in a coherent way 'the most advanced techniques of composition' with modified versions of historically received musical forms.[49] Since music is inherently historical, it is a mere illusion to pretend one could ignore the history of forms and start afresh. Applying this to Berg, Adorno writes: 'Allowing the ruptures between the modern and the late romantic to stand is more appropriate than trying to let music begin absolutely *ab ovo;* if music attempted this, it would fall prey to a past that was not understood and overcome'.[50]

Berg's Violin Concerto presented a particular problem for Adorno in this context.[51] He obviously found it deeply embarrassing and felt the need to explain it away by referring to the fact that Berg had had to compose it to commission with uncharacteristic haste; thus it didn't really represent his work at its best.[52] What really bothered Adorno was not the continued presence of some traditional elements (e.g. of tonal centres): this can be seen as a novel (i.e. 'new') appropriation of the tradition and hence an expression of the 'truth' that music is embedded in history. Nor even was it the 'ruptures of style' ('Stilbrüche') involved in the use of the Bach chorale; though Adorno writes that he doesn't want to 'defend' these, they too could in principle be dealt with as forms of honest recognition of historical discontinuity.[53] What Adorno couldn't tolerate was above all the easy comprehensibility of the work and its resulting popularity, for in a world as pervasively evil as Adorno thought ours was, the 'truth' would have to be highly esoteric.[54] Furthermore, the Violin Concerto seemed to be an 'affirmative' work in the traditional sense, one that cast an aesthetic glow of consolation over pain and fostered a metaphysical acceptance of death. It followed, he said with ironic reference to Richard Strauss, a scheme of 'Death and Transfiguration'.[55]

I do not find Adorno's treatment of Berg's relation to history and tradition very satisfactory, and the inadequacies of his account are, I think, deeply rooted in his general philosophical approach. Adorno does point out some of the retrograde forms that occur in Berg's music – he could hardly have failed to mention them, given that Berg himself explicitly draws attention to them[56] – but he fails to give these circular and retrograde forms the prominence in his analysis they deserve. One might even think that there could be a natural affinity between large-scale retrograde forms and the principle of 'construction/deconstruction' on which Berg's mature works, according to Adorno, are based.

As Robert Morgan points out, the prevalence of these retrograde and circular forms seems to be connected with a basically cyclical conception of time.[57] For Adorno, as for the Hegelian–Marxist tradition in aesthetics out of which his work arose, the threefold distinction between fundamentally ahistorical, fundamentally linear-progressive and fundamentally cyclical views of time and history is of central philosophical, aesthetic and political significance. The late nineteenth-century bourgeoisie which (correctly) feels itself threatened by the rising proletariat must give up its ideology of inevitable progress and retreat from history either into the timeless present of 'positivism' – this is, as it were, the 'soft' Western liberal option – or, when the going really gets tough, into cyclical or other mythic forms of historical thought – this is the proto-fascist option. To protect Berg's progressivist credentials, it was thus highly politic for Adorno to understate the importance of circular and cyclical forms. To be sure, Adorno rejects not just 'positivism' and 'mythic' thought, but also eighteenth- and nineteenth-century 'linear' conceptions in which an underlying 'logic of history' guarantees inevitable progress. There is, Adorno thinks, no guarantee of such 'progress' – at least if that means moral progress or progress in the quality of art. From the fact that the 'modern' artist confronts what are in some sense more stringent historical demands (made by the material) than previous artists did, it does not follow that 'new' art will necessarily be 'better' than older forms of art were. It is central to

Adorno's project that this kind of *internal* criticism of Enlightenment views of historical progress should *not* be taken to imply a
reversion to any of the archaic modes of thought which are the
natural precursors (and concomitants) of fascism;[58] a metaphysical view of time as circular would be one such archaic
conception.

In principle, Adorno could have tried to argue 'dialectically'
that Berg was showing that in our world, as modern barbarism
grew (in the 1930s), time was circular. In presenting our world
in this way Berg would not be making a metaphysical claim,
but a tacit (and correct) quasi-empirical criticism of our society
(as it looks in the light of a redeemed messianic future), and in
this sense his music could be called 'true'.[59] The Third Reich
was in some sense the archaic past *redivivus*. Lacking, however,
the fixed points which Hegel's dialectic still retains – a system of
logical categories and an affirmative relation to at least some
basic features of contemporary society – Adorno's 'negative
dialectics' can easily come to seem not the expression of a free,
sophisticated cognitive subjectivity, but a form of special
pleading.

Adorno would have no truck with astrology, numerology,
the occult, or any of the theories of a biologically based life-
rhythm that were popular among the members of the Schönberg circle.[60] He thought belief in such things a sign of rigidity,
conformism, depersonalisation and a predisposition to proto-
fascist attitudes.[61] What seems to have bothered him about
numerology and astrology was their pretence to scientific
standing, for Adorno himself had no objection in principle to
trying to 'read' the meaning of things or people from their
appearance. Onomastics and physiognomy, if carried out in
conjunction with an informed experience of *'Geist'* (and if
dispensing with any claim to objectivity), were perfectly acceptable; so were psychoanalytic interpretations. Thus Adorno
refers Wagner's ungenerous characterisation of Mime in *Siegfried* to the composer's fear at recognising part of himself in

Mime: Wagner, too, had a large head, was virtually a dwarf and talked too much.[62] Adorno also emphasises that Berg was 'like' his name: he was tall and gaunt like an alpine landscape ('Berg') and also elegantly old-fashioned and Catholic ('Alban');[63] remarkably, this is a claim he made not just about Berg's person, but also about his music.[64]

Indeed, despite the great documentary value of Adorno's recollections of Berg and the occasional brilliance of his analyses, the work on Berg is not one of the stronger parts of Adorno's œuvre. The reason for this that immediately suggests itself is that Adorno's negative dialectics work best when pointing out why, for one reason or another, a certain kind of artistic project is doomed to failure. As I have shown, at the deeper reaches of Adorno's philosophising, Berg's work is obliterated altogether, along with virtually all of twentieth-century music (except perhaps a handful of pieces from Schönberg's period of free atonality), but assuming one does not follow the dialectic out that far, the project of analysing relative failure and success remains. Occasionally Adorno's animosity is too overwhelming, as in the case of Wagner,[65] or his fear is too great – what if, after all, Stravinsky and not Schönberg was the representative of truly 'new' music? – and then the gears of the dialectical machinery can fail to engage, but in the case of Berg it seems instead to be Adorno's genuine love of his subject and his desire to present Berg's work as a great aesthetic success that get the better of him.

### NOTES

1 Theodor W. Adorno, *GS* 13, i.e. vol. 13 of *Gesammelte Schriften,* ed. G. Adorno and R. Tiedemann (Frankfurt: Suhrkamp, 1970–), p. 340.
2 See Jan Maegard, 'Zu Th. W. Adornos Rolle im Mann/Schönberg Streit', in R. Wiecker (ed.), *Gedenkschrift für Thomas Mann 1875–1975* (Copenhagen: Verlag Text und Kontext, 1975), pp. 216–17. Admittedly this is a retrospective judgement and Schönberg was not always the most fair-minded judge. See also Thomas Mann's letter

to Jonas Lesser of 15 October 1951 (*Briefe*, ed. E. Mann, vol. 3 [Frankfurt: Fischer, 1965], pp. 225–8); also Jürgen Habermas's two essays on Adorno in *Philosophisch-Politische Profile* (Frankfurt: Suhrkamp, 1971).

3 *The Berg–Schönberg Correspondence*, p. 335; Adorno, *GS* 13, p. 361.

4 An early account of Adorno's compositions is René Leibowitz, 'Der Komponist Theodor W. Adorno', in M. Horkheimer (ed.), *Zeugnisse: Theodor W. Adorno zum 60. Geburtstag* (Frankfurt: Europäische Verlagsanstalt, 1963), pp. 355–9; for more recent commentary see *Musik-Konzepte*, vols. 63–4, ed. H.-K. Metzger and R. Riehn (Munich: edition text+kritik, 1989) and the essay by Siegfried Schibli issued with the CD recording WER 6173–2 (Mainz: Wergo, 1990).

5 As late as 1938 he was writing that 'according to our theory there will be no war' (Adorno–Benjamin, *Briefwechsel, 1928–1940*, ed. H. Lonitz (Frankfurt: Suhrkamp, 1994), p. 328) and even in early 1939 he is not convinced that war will come (*ibid.*, pp. 388–90).

6 Leo Löwenthal, 'Erinnerungen an Adorno', in L. von Friedeburg and J. Habermas (eds.), *Adorno-Konferenz 1983* (Frankfurt: Suhrkamp, 1983), p. 390.

7 Reich, *Alban Berg*, pp. 21–7 ('Klaviersonate, op. 1'), pp. 27–31 ('Vier Lieder, op. 2'), pp. 31–5 ('Sieben frühe Lieder'), pp. 35–43 ('Streichquartett, op. 3'), pp. 47–52 ('Vier Stücke für Klarinette und Klavier'), pp. 52–64 ('Drei Orchesterstücke, op. 6'), pp. 91–101 ('Lyrische Suite für Streichquartett'), pp. 101–6 ('Konzertarie "Der Wein"').

8 Wiesengrund began publishing essays under the name 'Theodor Wiesengrund-Adorno' in the 1930s, but people who knew him continued to refer to him and address him as 'Wiesengrund'. Berg refers to him exclusively in this way. By 1943 he is 'Dr. Adorno' (see Thomas Mann, *Die Entstehung des 'Doktor Faustus'* (Frankfurt: Fischer, 1949), pp. 31–5 *et passim*).

9 Adorno, *Philosophie der neuen Musik* (Tübingen: J. C. B. Mohr, 1949). Eng. trans. of 2nd edn (Frankfurt: Europäische Verlagsanstalt, 1958) as *Philosophy of Modern Music*, trans. A. G. Mitchell and W. V. Blomster (London: Sheed and Ward, 1973). Repr. as vol. 12 of *GS*.

10 Mann describes the writing of the novel and his relations with Adorno in great detail in *Die Entstehung des 'Doktor Faustus'*.

11 Adorno, *GS* 18, pp. 488, 491; *GS* 13, p. 402. Both Berg and Leverkühn find it difficult to focus their general aesthetic interests and

confine them to music, both are interested in numerology, etc. Mann adds that in both the real music of Berg and the imaginary music of Leverkühn dissonance is the expression of the serious and spiritual, while harmony and tonality (*'das Harmonische und Tonale'*) stand for hell or the world of the commonplace (Mann, *Tagebücher*, ed. P. Mendelssohn and I. Jens, 9 vols. (Frankfurt: Fischer, 1979–93), *1946*, p. 769). None of this really amounts to much.

12 *'Die Deitschen fressen immer nur Dreck'* (Adorno, *GS* 18, p. 489); cf. *GS* 13, p. 340, *GS* 20, p. 553.

13 Leverkühn rejects the tempting offers of the French impresario Fittelsberg to enter 'le grand monde', maintains his artistic integrity and stays put in his rural retreat. Berg didn't imagine that a concert in Paris would threaten his integrity: he gave one in 1928 (see Jarman, *The Music of Alban Berg*, p. 10 n. 2). A few more such performances in the 1930s would have allowed Berg to buy an even more powerful car. It is hard to imagine Leverkühn buying a car.

14 Mann, *Tagebücher, 1949–1950*, p. 580.

15 Adorno's end was as grotesque, in its way, as those of Berg, Webern and Schönberg. Throughout the 1950s and early 1960s he had kept up a steady stream of social and cultural criticism, but he seems to have been surprised by the German student movement of the mid- and late 1960s and quickly distanced himself from it. A number of incidents – such as his public handshake with the burly police chief who organised the removal of students occupying his Institute for Social Research – caused consternation among members of the left. Finally, a group of women students decided to stage an 'Adorno love-in'. Stripping to the waist, they performed a parody of the Flower Maidens scene from *Parsifal*, dancing in an erotically suggestive way around Adorno as he entered the lecture-hall and pelting him with flowers. This was an extremely astute tactic. Adorno prided himself on not being a prude, but the 'love-in' was too much for him. Shielding his eyes from the sight of the women's breasts with his leather briefcase, he left the lecture-hall – without (for once) speaking. He left for a holiday in Switzerland without trying to lecture again and died there of a heart-attack.

16 For a good full-length treatment of Adorno's views on art see Susan Buck-Morss, *The Origin of Negative Dialectics: Theodor W. Adorno, Walter Benjamin, and the Frankfurt Institute* (New York: Macmillan, 1977). The best discussion of Adorno's theory of music is

Max Paddison, *Adorno's Aesthetics of Music* (Cambridge: Cambridge University Press, 1993). See also Raymond Geuss, review of Adorno's *Aesthetic Theory, Journal of Philosophy* (1986), pp. 732–41.

17 See the last section of the final poem ('Le Voyage') in Baudelaire's *Les Fleurs du mal.*

18 See W. Benjamin, 'Zentralpark', in *Illuminationen* (Frankfurt: Suhrkamp, 1977), p. 247.

19 There might seem to be strong similarities between these views of Adorno and those held by Schönberg. Schönberg, too, rejects the idea that the artist is trying to realise beauty, and claims that art must be 'true' ('Die Kunst soll nicht schmücken sondern wahr sein', Willi Reich, *Arnold Schönberg oder Der konservative Revolutionär* (Vienna: Fritz Molden Verlag, 1968), p. 44; cf. Adorno, *GS* 18, p. 62). Schönberg also gives a central place to the 'necessity' of artistic production (see *Harmonielehre,* 3rd rev. edn (Vienna: Universal Edition, 1922), chapter 22; *Stil und Gedanke: Aufsätze zur Musik,* ed. I. Vojtech [Frankfurt: Fischer, 1976], p. 73). However, when Schönberg speaks of 'truth' he usually seems to have in mind authenticity of expression, that a musically elaborated form of an original inspiration (*'Einfall'*) is *true to* that *'Einfall'* and hence an authentic expression of the composer (*Stil und Gedanke,* p. 6). This notion of truth of expression is completely different from Adorno's Hegelian idea of 'truth'. For Adorno, the expressionist self and its *'Einfälle'* are not the absolute to which art must be true (*GS* 12, p. 52). Crudely put, the composer may have a worthless *'Einfall',* and an authentic elaboration of it won't make it a work of art. Similarly, when Schönberg speaks of 'necessity' he seems usually to mean the composer's inner need for self-expression, not the necessity of a particular solution to the puzzle the material presents. On freedom and necessity see Adorno's two essays 'Reaktion und Fortschritt' (*GS* 16) and 'Stilgeschichte in Schönbergs Werk' (*GS* 18), both from the 1930s.

20 Adorno, *GS* 12, pp. 13–19.

21 Stravinsky's published comments on political matters over the course of a long lifetime present a no less contradictory picture than do his remarks on many other matters. In the 1930s and 1940s he seems to have had little time for Hitler but quite a lot of time for Mussolini and some sympathy for Franco, though his words and actions are perhaps easier to reconcile with an instinct for self-preservation than with a strong and consistent political

stance. See 'Stravinsky's Politics', in Vera Stravinsky and Robert Craft (eds.), *Stravinsky in Pictures and Documents* (New York: Simon and Schuster, 1978), pp. 547–58. [Ed.]

22 In the 'Preface' to *Philosophie der neuen Musik,* Adorno states that the book can be seen as an 'excursus' to *Dialektik der Aufklärung,* a book he wrote jointly with Max Horkheimer in the early 1940s.

23 The most concise and accessible account of this work is in David Held's *Introduction to Critical Theory: Horkheimer to Habermas* (Berkeley: University of California Press, 1980), chapter 5; see also Paul Connerton, *The Tragedy of Enlightenment: An Essay on the Frankfurt School* (Cambridge: Cambridge University Press, 1980).

24 It is precisely this that Schönberg seems to want to deny by denying that there is a twelve-note system and insisting that he had invented a method or technique: 'One must follow the series; but nevertheless one composes as freely as before' ('*Man muss der Grundreihe folgen; aber trotzdem komponiert man so frei wie zuvor*', *Stil und Gedanke,* p. 80). Schönberg always said that Adorno had missed the point (see his letter of 27 July 1932 to Rudolf Kolisch: *Stil und Gedanke,* p. 150). Adorno tries to defend himself in the '*Vorrede*' to his *Moments Musicaux* (in *GS* 16). If the method of composing with twelve notes related only to each other is *just* a method and 'not the only route to the solution of the new problems' (Maegard, 'Zu Th. W. Adornos Rolle', p. 218) then one of the main assumptions of *Philosophie der neuen Musik* is undermined. Note that there is another (and much less plausible) version of Schönberg's famous dictum, namely: 'One follows the series, but composes just as before' ('*Man folgt der Grundreihe, komponiert aber im übrigen wie zuvor*'). Twelve-note composition might well be 'just as free' as tonal composition, but it is very hard to believe it can be just like it.

25 Adorno, *Philosophy of Modern Music,* pp. 68–9. *GS* 12: '*Das Subjekt gebietet über die Musik durchs rationale System, um selbst dem rationalen System zu erliegen.*' (p. 68); '*Die neue Ordnung der Zwölftontechnik löscht virtuell das Subjekt aus.*' (p. 70).

26 Adorno, *GS* 14, p. 9.

27 Adorno, *GS* 12, pp. 122–6.

28 Adorno, *GS* 18, p. 668. Note that Adorno is constantly praising Berg's 'economy' (e.g. *GS* 18, p. 462).

29 Adorno, *Philosophy of Modern Music,* p. 30. '*Die einzigen Werke heute, die zählen, sind die, welche keine Werke mehr sind.*' *GS* 12, p. 37.

30 For details see Jarman, *Alban Berg: Lulu,* chapters 1 and 2.

31 Including, apparently, Schönberg (*The Berg–Schönberg Correspondence,* p. 365).

32 'I cannot say with certainty whether it is I who first pointed him toward *Lulu,* as it now seems to me upon reflection; in such cases it is easy to err out of narcissism' (*Alban Berg,* p. 26). This is so uncharacteristically modest one might be tempted to think there is something to it. In any case since we know that Berg attended a performance of *Die Büchse der Pandora* in 1905, almost twenty years before he first met Adorno (who, after all was only born in 1903), Adorno can at most imply that he drew Berg's attention to the operatic possibilities of a play which the composer already knew well.

33 Given Berg's evident fascination with ways in which music can emerge gradually from noise (see Adorno, *GS* 13, pp. 416–21; also Perle, *Wozzeck,* p. 10) it is a shame that we will never hear Pippa's musical glass.

34 See Adorno–Benjamin, *Briefwechsel,* p. 398.

35 Repr. in Jarman, *Alban Berg: Wozzeck,* p. 138.

36 Repr. in *ibid.,* p. 156.

37 See Perle, *Wozzeck,* pp. 25–37.

38 Adorno, *GS* 12, p. 37.

39 Adorno, *GS* 16, p. 94: 'jedes Stück Bergs war seiner Unmöglichkeit abgelistet'.

40 Adorno, *GS* 12, p. 37.

41 Friedrich Cerha, 'Some Further Notes on my Realization of Act III of *Lulu*', in Jarman (ed.), *The Berg Companion,* pp. 261–7.

42 Adorno, *GS* 13, p. 452.

43 Adorno, *GS* 18, p. 458, 654; *GS* 13, pp. 325–30.

44 Adorno, *GS* 18, pp. 667–70; cf. *GS* 13, p. 355.

45 Adorno, *GS* 13, p. 440.

46 Adorno, *GS* 18, pp. 467, 475; *GS* 16, pp. 88–90.

47 See Nietzsche's discussion of 'active' and 'passive' pessimism in *Der Wille zur Macht,* ed. P. Gast and E. Förster-Nietzsche (Stuttgart: Kröner, 1964), pp. 10–96.

48 Adorno, *GS* 13, p. 346.

49 Adorno, *GS* 18, p. 461; *GS* 16, pp. 90–6. This, of course, is just what Boulez objects to in his early essay '*Incidences actuelles de Berg*' (1948) – Boulez playing Baudelaire, as it were, to Adorno's Hegel (Eng. trans. as 'The Current Impact of Berg [the Fortnight of Aus-

trian Music in Paris]: in *Stocktakings from an Apprenticeship,* trans. S. Walsh [Oxford: Clarendon, 1991], pp. 183–7).

50 Adorno, *GS* 18, p. 500: *'Das Stehen-Lassen der Brüche zwischen Moderne und Spätromantik ist angemessener als begänne die Musik absolut von vorn; eben damit fiele sie dem undurchschauten Gewesenen zur Beute.'*
51 See Pople, *Berg: Violin Concerto,* pp. 98–9.
52 Adorno, *GS* 18, p. 500; *GS* 13, p. 350; *GS* 15, p. 340.
53 Adorno, *GS* 18, pp. 499–501; *GS* 13, p. 349. Contrast this again with Boulez's 'The Current Impact of Berg'.
54 Adorno, *GS* 16, p. 86.
55 Adorno, *GS* 18, p. 500; cf. *ibid.,* pp. 667–70.
56 For instance in the open letter to Schönberg about the Chamber Concerto (Eng. trans. in Reich, *Life and Work,* pp. 143–8, and in *The Berg–Schönberg Correspondence,* pp. 334–7).
57 Robert P. Morgan, 'The Eternal Return: Retrograde and Circular Form in Berg', in Gable and Morgan (eds.), *Alban Berg,* pp. 111–49.
58 Adorno, *GS* 12, p. 10.
59 Adorno, *GS* 4, p. 281; *GS* 12, pp. 122–6.
60 See Douglas Jarman, 'Alban Berg, Wilhelm Fliess, and the Secret Programme of the Violin Concerto', in Jarman (ed.), *The Berg Companion,* pp. 181–94.
61 Adorno, 'Aberglaube aus zweiter Hand', in *GS* 8, pp. 147–76.
62 Adorno, *GS* 13, pp. 22–3.
63 *Ibid.,* pp. 342–3.
64 *Ibid.,* p. 347. Oddly enough, Adorno, who throughout his life was known to his friends as 'Teddie', was also very much 'like' his name. If Berg was an alpine chapel, the short, stout Adorno, who spoke continuously in an over-articulated voice, was an animated teddy-bear, who kept trying to cover himself in as many glittering ornaments as possible.
65 Adorno admits this to Benjamin (see Adorno–Benjamin, *Briefwechsel,* pp. 344–5).

# 6

## FORM AND 'THE NEW' IN ADORNO'S
## *'VERS UNE MUSIQUE INFORMELLE'*

### I

IN 1961 Adorno gave an invited lecture at Darmstadt with the title *'Vers une musique informelle'*. This lecture, which was published later in the same year in the *Darmstädter Beiträge*,[1] was intended and received as an intervention in a specific contemporary debate that had been taking place in the centres of compositional activity about the future of music. Roughly speaking this was a debate between proponents of one or another version of 'serialism' (e.g. Boulez and Stockhausen), who proposed to develop certain tendencies they found instantiated in the Schönberg of the 'twelve-tone' period into a system of complete unification of all aspects of a piece of music according to a single principle and the iconoclastic attempts by John Cage to break with the tradition of increasing rationalization by introducing aleatory elements and noise into music. Adorno's talk is an attempt not just to describe what kind of future music might have (if any), but to recommend to composers a particular direction in which Adorno believes they ought to move in this historical situation.

We're used to ways of thinking about art in general that mix historical, stylistic, and evaluative categories. Thus there is the older contrast between 'the ancients' and 'the moderns' and later distinctions between 'classic' and 'Romantic' or 'Romantic' and 'modern(ist)'. What is first striking about Adorno's theory of music is his failure to see any serious discontinuity in its development during the past 200 years.[2] It isn't that during that period there have been no changes at all in the way music was composed or that the criteria of what counts as a good piece of music have stayed exactly the same. Obviously they have changed in any number of important ways, but, he believes, from a sufficient distance the whole development can be seen as an internal unfolding of some basic assumptions that were there from the very beginning.[3] From Haydn to Darmstadt (and beyond) composers have been seeking to write works that are formally new, i.e. that exhibit originality of form. Good music is new music and the best music is music that exhibits a *new* kind of form. The creation of new kinds of significant form, he claims, was both the object of aspiration of composers and the basic criterion or standard for evaluating the success or failure of a musical work. I want now to look in some detail at each of the two components in this standard, first the notion of the *'new'*, and then the notion of '(significant) form'.

The first of these two components is that a musical composition in order to be successful must be *new* – it must be original, different in kind from what went before, an expression of a fresh way of doing things, a fresh perception, etc. Adorno sometimes connects this with the demands of the bourgeois market. A feudal society may value ritualistic, highly stylized, repetitive forms of art, but a commercial society values novelty, and this valuation eventually moves from the marketplace into the aesthetic sphere itself. This notion of 'novelty' ('originality') is often connected with some notion of freedom, of breaking out or emancipating oneself from stodgy, pre-given, fixed, merely conventional kinds of expression on the other.[4] Thus in his essay *'Neue Musik, veraltete Musik, Stil und Gedanke'* (*Stil und Gedanke*, p. 26), Schönberg says essentially that the only valuable music is music that expresses something original: *'Kunst heißt neue Kunst'* i.e. 'All *art* [i.e. art as opposed to mere conventional, everyday routine communication] is *new* art'. This is often associated with the liberal (and Romantic) assumption that since each of us is a unique individual, if we were free and capable we would each express ourselves in a way that would be original and unique. A composer, then, who was good, would be someone who was free and able adequately to express himself or herself in a way which would be authentically unique and thus radically 'new'. Adorno very specifically associates himself with this demand and in fact emphasizes that his preferred term for referring to the twentieth-century music which he considered serious was '*new* music' *rather* than '*modern* music', i.e. what was important about it was not its place in a historical sequence, but its inherent aesthetic property of unexpectedness and originality (cf. '*Musik und neue Musik*', *GS* 16.476ff.).

When Adorno speaks of the 'category' of 'the new' (e.g. *ÄT* 40) he is using the term 'category' in the specifically Hegelian sense, according to which a 'category' is something relative to which the distinction between subjective and objective doesn't apply. Categories are *equally* forms of 'objects' in the world and forms of our way of conceptualizing things in the world. So 'the new' can't be defined either exclusively by reference to any existing 'objective' features, or ways in which something differs from what has gone before, nor exclusively by reference to a subjective reaction of surprise, shock, amazement, etc. which persons might experience in the encounter with a work of art, but must be seen as referring to '(objectively) different properties of the world (or of a work of art) that are experienced as novel'.

The second demand is that the successful work must exhibit some aesthetically significant form. Adorno doesn't himself actually use the term 'significant form' *per se* – it is taken from Clive Bell[5] – but he does speak of form and 'sense' as roughly alternative ways to speak, and so I think it legitimate to put the two together in the way I have (cf. use of '*der musikalische Sinn*', *GS* 16.539). Adorno connects this notion of significant form with cognition in two ways. First of all, the form is significant only if it can be recognized. A successful piece of music can't be *so* relentlessly hermetic that it is in principle impossible for potential auditors to hear the piece 'from the inside' with understanding at all (although, of course, there might well be significant features that weren't audible and comprehensible even to well-trained auditors even on repeated hearings). Second, a significant form is one that enlightens us about some fundamental features of our world, our society, and our life (in addition, of course, to what it tells us about all previous music). It doesn't, of course, 'enlighten' us by formulating or communicating a distinct propositional content, but it must, Adorno thinks, be seen in the context of trying to come to terms cognitively with our world and society. That is, art has a certain autonomy – in the modern period it follows its own laws that are not simply dictated to it by some other authority (such as the Church) – but it also isn't, or at least shouldn't be, 'self-contained' and sheerly self-referential. Rather for Adorno a significant work of art must have what he calls a 'truth content' (*Wahrheitsgehalt*).[6] This notion of the 'truth content' of a work of art is inherently extremely obscure but it is absolutely central to his theory. This 'truth', which doesn't and can't have strictly propositional form, is in one sense always the same for all works of art, just as, Adorno says (*ÄT* 193), the answer to the question of the Sphinx is always the same: Our society deserves to be criticized for failure to live up to utopian expectations which it could in principle fulfil. One major difficulty for Adorno's view is how to put together these two ideas, first that art is autonomous and second that it shouldn't just have wider social and cultural (and political) 'significance' but should specifically tell a critical truth about our society. Works of art are ideally trying to instantiate an original and unique, 'new' kind of form, which they give themselves, while *thereby* criticizing society. The form of the work of art is both an original self-given configuration *and* the vehicle of profound social criticism.[7] Adorno would have been very resistant to the idea that this conjunction of aesthetic autonomy and social criticism was an accidental, historically specific conjunct of the situation in Vienna – and to perhaps a lesser extent *Mitteleuropa* in general – in the period between 1890 and 1940, and that the attempt to hold on to it was a mere expression of nostalgia for a retrospectively idealized past. If this historical analysis is correct, Adorno would have thought that simply one further sign of how far the modern world had fallen, and how much *more* in need of appropriate criticism it was. That seems fair enough.

Adorno's basic claim is that this set of (two) demands is and was always inherently incompatible, or contradictory, although historically this has not always been clear to artists and members of the general public. The development of art in the second half of the twentieth century has brought this contradiction closer to consciousness, but the contradiction was always at least latently present since the mid-eighteenth century. If the very notion of 'form' implies that of something that could at least in principle be recognized, then a work that had a 'form' would have to exhibit some discernible structural features that could in principle be connected with features and forms that are already familiar to the auditors. This has sometimes been thought to be a fact about the human possibilities of comprehension in that it has been claimed that to understand something is to reduce unfamiliar aspects of it to something familiar. However, if the work in question exhibits an order which is discernible or recognizable in this way, that will mean that it isn't really *fully* new, because recognition of the order it exhibits would require assimilation to pre-existing patterns. Anything really new wouldn't be comprehensible – and thus wouldn't really be art (because it is inherent to art that it be comprehended) – and anything that was comprehensible wouldn't really be new.

This line of thought might be thought to rest on a relatively elementary confusion between a) the claim that any work in order to be comprehensible must *presuppose* some pre-existing patterns and b) the claim that no work can *instantiate in any*

144

*important respect* any but pre-existing forms.[8] I take it, though, that Adorno would wish to deny that a sharp distinction can be drawn between these two theses and that he thinks that the relatively simple set of considerations outlined in the last paragraph means that art faces an irreconcilable dilemma; it must opt for 'comprehensibility' at the price of lack of 'newness' and hence artistic failure (if all good art must in fact be 'new' art), or for a 'newness' that by its very nature resists comprehension (but art that is incomprehensible, that really has no possible audience, is not art). In a sense all art, at least all post–eighteenth-century art, is a necessary failure, at best an attempt to snatch a kind of partial (and perhaps moral) victory out of the underlying defeat which is built into the very idea of art (at any rate since the mid-eighteenth century), and the increasingly conscious and clear recognition of this underlying dilemma itself contributes to making the dilemma more difficult to negotiate. I speak here advisedly of a 'moral' victory because another strand in Adorno's work emphasises the intention over the full and complete execution of the intention in new music: *'Das Neue ist die Sehnsucht nach dem Neuen, kaum es selbst, daran krankt alles Neue'* (*ÄT* 55).[9] The 'debility' of the 'new' (*woran es krankt*) is presumably not just the impossibility of creating any work of art that is wholly new, and the inherent evanescence, as Adorno calls it in another context, the rapid 'aging' of any 'new' form of art,[10] but the fact that no work of art, no matter how successful in its own terms, can be more than a *'promesse de bonheur'* not *'bonheur'* itself.[11] *'Bonheur'* itself couldn't be rendered accessible by any means short of radical social change.

II

I would like to make three points about Adorno's method in this tract. First of all, a 'dialectical' method of the kind he uses was traditionally understood – or at least 'was understood by

Hegel' – to be *essentially* retrospective and contemplative. It could, it was thought, give understanding of the present (in terms of the past which brought this present forth) but could not be used for historical predictions. Marx and the Young Hegelians tried to transform it into something that could be used predictively, but it isn't at all obvious that this is really possible. In particular dialectical philosophy could not be used for giving directions about how to act. Dialectic was precisely *not* supposed to be a form of *'Besserwisserei'*.[12] Philosophy gets its start when Socrates discovers that shoemakers in some sense don't know what they are doing,[13] but by the nineteenth century philosophers had come to realize that philosophy won't improve shoemakers' practice (although it might well do various other non-contemptible things). On the other hand, an aesthetic manifesto is essentially practical and prospective (not speculative and retrospective): it precisely is an attempt to encourage artists to discover or embark on a particular future path, to tell shoemakers how to make better shoes. There is something *inherently* odd about Adorno's project in *'Vers une musique informelle'* of using this dialectical method to tell us where music must, could, might, or ought to go. Strictly speaking, a Hegelian dialectician should claim that the 'outcome' of a conflict, tension, contradiction, etc. can be seen to be 'rational' or 'logical' *only retrospectively*.[14] As Kierkegaard says in criticizing Hegel, it is all very well to see that we can make sense of everything in the past dialectically as leading up to the present, but although we understand backwards, i.e. retrospectively, unfortunately we must live forwards. It is all very well to explain (from the vantage point of 1806 or 1998) to Antigone that the conflict between the divine unwritten laws of the family and the public reason of the city will be 'sublated' when the modern state integrates family, religion, and public law into a coherent integrated whole in which each component gets its due, but that won't help her. It will neither tell her what concretely she should do in her real situation – she must still decide that for herself – nor is it even clear that it will give her any kind of consolation beyond what she can in any case provide for herself from her own resources.[15] I would assume that the same would be true of contemporary music. If anything a dialectical understanding of its past would be an even less useful guide to how to compose than Hegel's *Phenomenology* would have been to Antigone because *ex hypothesi* the future 'resolution' is as yet not known to us. If that future was cognitively fully accessible to us, we wouldn't be in a predicament that required the writing of essays entitled *'Vers. . . . '*

Since this is an important point which it is easy to fail to grasp, I will pursue it now at somewhat greater length. It isn't, for Hegel, that we are (first) able to tell the coherent story of how the previous history of some human activity (such as art) leads up to the present as a fully rational and adequate realization of what was implicit in that past, and *then* the 'understanding' embodied in that story *dictates* to us what the necessary next step in the story will be. It is rather that *only* when we have succeeded in determining, as it were, on grounds *independent* of the historical story which will eventually be told by the dialectical philosopher, what the next step is to be, and only when we have made that step and seen that it is *successful* that we can *look back* and begin to tell the dialectical story of the prehistory of that success coherently. Concretely, no amount of internal dialectical study of the history of music in 1903 would have yielded a coherent story that would have forced the conclusion that composers *must* now try to abandon tonality in their works. Only when Schönberg has actually made the break and begun to compose successful atonal works, can he (and others) look back and see for the first time that what was actually going on in the late nineteenth century was the story of the exhaustion and terminal break-down of tonality; only then can they present the history of music from Haydn to 1914 as one of the gradual development and exhaustion of tonality and its replacement by 'atonal'[16] music as a unitary, coherent dialectical sequence. That 'the owl of Minerva takes flight only with the coming of dusk'[17] is part of what makes it possible to speak of the genuinely *'new'* in art. Schönberg *was* in one sense just drawing the natural conclusion from the history of music in the eighteenth and nineteenth centuries but one can *see* that that is the case only *after* he had successfully drawn the conclusion. 'Successfully' here means not just theoretically, but as embodied in successful works of art. The *aesthetic* success of Schönberg's music was part of what made it possible thereafter to write this dialectical coherent history; it is essential to the story that Schönberg's music was, as music, 'better' than that of the historically inconsequential Hauer.

Another way to put the same thing is that for a dialectic of the Hegelian kind to operate, one must be sure one can apply the category of 'totality', i.e. one must be sure one has *all* the relevant parts of the story. Looking back at the past (e.g. at Schönberg) from the present (e.g. from the standpoint of Adorno in the early 1960s) we can assume we have all the relevant parts, that the past forms a closed system. We can then show how the various tensions in the material find a certain kind of resolution (or *fail* to find resolution) in Schönberg's work. This is not true of the future; we don't *now* know we have all the relevant parts of *that* story, so the category of 'totality' doesn't obviously have correct application to what we have. In the future unexpected parts of the world that have previously stood *outside* the charmed circle of German-Austrian music from Bach (or Haydn) to Stockhausen might become relevant parts of the 'material', or technical devices (e.g. computers) might *add* possibilities to the material that were not antecedently there. To *assume* that we *do* have all relevant parts of the story and can apply the category of totality is to try to impose an unwarranted determinateness on a situation that may well be open.

In short there is an inherent tension between dialectics as an approach and Adorno's attempt to rehabilitate *'Ismen'* (*GS*

16.496) and give what amounts to an avant-garde manifesto of a new and as yet untried way of composing.[18] The retrospective, 'speculative' dialectical treatise and the prospective avant-garde manifesto are separate genres that don't really fit together.

Second, abstracting for a moment from the whole issue of the compatibility of dialectics and manifestos, Adorno's basic approach, focusing as it does on the internal development of the logic of music, makes the whole process impersonal in that the achievement of individual composers is not finally significant in determining the course of history – those composers are, of course, in one sense terribly important, but they are important because they are drawing out 'objective', almost logical consequences of tensions that exist in the *'Material'*. That means that, really, anyone who was sufficiently steeped in the tradition[19] and sufficiently musical would come to the same conclusion, more or less. I wonder if there isn't another way to think about this which has more to recommend it than Adorno admits. This is one I think of as deriving from Proust's discussion of late Beethoven (in *À l'ombre des jeunes filles en fleurs*). Here Proust emphasizes the way in which a great work of art creates its own audience, creates a need for itself. This might be thought to be compatible with Adorno's view because the creation of that need might be the next step in the elaboration of the internal logic of compositional history, but Proust goes out of his way to claim that it can be even *idiosyncratic* features of, say, Beethoven's music that can give rise to a need for *that kind of music*. Despite Adorno's claims about *'das kompositorische Subjekt'* and its freedom, I don't see that he takes adequate account of this.

If I understand it correctly, Adorno's theory of the freedom of the compositional subject runs as follows. He takes over from Hegel as his basic model that of a subject who stands in a dialectical relation to an object. At any historical period one can distinguish between what Adorno calls the *'material'* (this is the 'object-pole' of the dialectic relation) and what he calls *'das kompositorische Subjekt'* who is endowed with certain *'compositional forces of production'* (*kompositorische Produktivkräfte*). The *'material'* is, as Adorno repeatedly states, not a physical magnitude, but everything composers in the historical period in question have before them including pre-given forms (inherited from previous compositional activity): *'die Tonalität, die temperierte Skala, die Möglichkeit der Modulation in vollkommenem Quintenzirkel [und] . . . . ungezählte idiomatische Bestandteile [der] musikalische[n] Sprache'* (*GS* 16.503). The basic claim now is that this material *itself* has an inherent structure and tendency. It is, as it were, in motion in a certain direction at any given time. The material can be seen to be in motion because it is the sedimented result of previous compositional activity including the unfulfilled aspirations of previous composers (in the face of what they were able to accomplish with the historical material which they had at their disposal). Now *if* the composers in question have fully developed compositional forces, this will be partly because they have fully internalized the traditional material and associated practices, expectations, aesthetic predilections, etc. and this means that their own *spontaneous* reactions to the material will themselves 'naturally' run in the direction of the 'tendency' of the material itself. In this happy state there will be a conformity between the inherent tendencies of the 'material', what the 'material' requires or demands (roughly, 'objective' necessity) and what composers spontaneously want (roughly, subjective freedom). Doing what the material demands will not be experienced as conforming to external coercion or pressure, but as acting on one's own inmost spontaneous impulses; in this state, then, the composing subject will attain Hegelian freedom, finding itself 'at-home' in its 'other', the material.

I merely note that Adorno seems to vacillate slightly between two different formulations here that are not obviously synonymous. Sometimes he speaks of the 'tendency' of the material, sometimes of the 'demands' of the material.[20] The first of these is compatible with allowing for *alternative* potentially equally possible responses – if, to take a crude example, the material has a tendency in the direction of tighter organization of large-scale forms, there might be a variety of different formal ways of achieving that. However, to speak of the 'demands' or 'requirements' of the material suggests very strongly that the material poses an utterly determinate question to which there is and can be only one determinate answer (all others being incorrect). When Adorno describes certain forms of traditional composition as like trying to solve a puzzle, or when he speaks of art as a 'riddle', this determinateness is conceived as maximal. With a puzzle there is usually only *one* pre-determined way in which the pieces can fit together, and a 'riddle' usually has an answer.[21]

Does the 'musical material' just exhibit 'tendencies' or does it actually pose distinct sharply formulated questions to which there are uniquely well-formed answers? Is the composer discovering the pre-given answer to a riddle the material has posed or inventing/constructing a work in a way that accommodates the inherent tendencies of the work, but represents only one possible accommodation of that set of tendencies? Is composition more like solving a cross-word puzzle or more like solving a task in engineering where a number of different demands – stability, simplicity, efficiency, etc. – have all to be respected and there may be no pre-given optimal ordering of them and no uniquely good way of satisfying them all at once? If the composer is more like the engineer, there is room for the Proustian vision. Is it obvious that the composer becomes *freer* the more the task is like solving the cross-word puzzle?

One must not, then, be naive in trying to say what the material at any given time *is*. It may not just be unclear whether the material at a given time asks a determinate question to which the determinate, uniquely correct answer must be found, but part of the task may be precisely to decide or determine (or discover – which way of putting it is correct?) what the material *is*. Again Adorno seems to vacillate between two different ways of understanding the 'material'. One is a Hegelian way – the 'material' is what is pre-given to the individual composer by history; composers do not choose it any more than they choose to be born at a certain time and place. It is just there. What it is is given by an objective aesthetic *Geschichtsphilosophie*. Note, too, that to say that the material is there already is not *just* to say that composers must start to work from pre-existing things. Rather the material is normatively or peremptorily there. It is what (historically) *demands* attention. The second is a phenomenological use of the term 'material' which starts from the actual experience of composers.[22] They do choose a certain material to work on, a set of themes, a row, a set of parameters, and these in some sense pre-exist the compositional process. 'Material' is, as Adorno defines it at other places, 'what the composer operates with. . . . everything which stands over opposite them and about which they must make a decision'.[23] It is an important feature of Adorno's view that a composer can in one sense choose to work on the *wrong* kind of material, i.e. the chosen material in the phenomenological sense may not be the material that is historically required. There is not just a *'Zwang des Materials'*, a 'coercion' the given 'material' exercises (once it is, as it were, 'chosen'), but *also* a *'Zwang zu spezifischem Material'* (*ÄT* 222), i.e. a historical necessity which forces a composer who wishes to write significant music to work on and with specific material. That is, one *can* chose to operate on kinds of things that are historically irrelevant – that are not part of the pre-given, historically mandatory material. One can try to answer questions history doesn't ask, but whatever internal aesthetic properties the results of this undertaking may have, they won't be great art. Adorno also would probably believe that the irrelevance of the question would influence the inherent aesthetic properties of the reply in deleterious ways, but that is a separate issue.

Another way to put this is that in the phenomenological sense, the 'material' is a prospective judgment – the composer has it, knows what it is, and proposes to work on it. In a sense to speak of the 'material' in the *geschichtsphilosophisch* sense is to make a retrospective judgment. We can only see what the material *was* – what the question was – when we have seen the answer. A great composer is one who can be seen in retrospect to have defined in a particular way what the material was at that historical juncture. Defining what the material (in the *geschichtsphilosophisch* sense) is/was isn't a prelude to composition, but an integral part of it, in some sense perhaps the most important part, just as in philosophy it can be thought to be more important to have seen or defined what the question is than to have given any particular answer to that question.

It is this claim about the determinateness of question and answer that allows Adorno to deploy the whole apparatus of 'Verbindlichkeit', truth and falsity, 'Zwang', logic, necessity, etc. Of course, Adorno is careful to reject the implausible suggestion that the existing material is *both* pre-given and *simply* dictates in an univocal way how it is to be composed: *'[Die Form] . . . ist nicht mehr . . . aus Autonomie zu erzeugen, souverän zu planen; genauso wenig aber ist sie aus dem Material herauszulesen, das . . . als Götze sich aufrichtete'.*[24] This, he recognizes, would be tantamount to the imposition of an inappropriate and excessive kind of 'objectivity' on the compositional process. Composition isn't really like finding the last piece in a jig-saw puzzle. Still, however, he insists that a musical composition must exhibit a *necessity* of succession – *'Die Notwendigkeit dieser und keiner anderen Zeitfolge'*[25] which is not derived from any extra-musical sources. What I want to suggest is that *either* this view is uninformative, asserting no more than that composition must use some pre-given material which imposes some constraints on the composer, but that the composer must form that material in some way that the material itself does not strictly dictate, *or*, if the use of the apparatus of 'dialectic' and its associated notions (especially 'necessity') is *serious*, it may actually introduce the *illusion* of a determinateness that does not exist and mask the need for choice.

Note that it may well be a (virtually) necessary illusion for a particular composer in a particular historical situation or even for all composers in that period to think that there *is* a determinate answer to some question the material poses. Being in thrall to this illusion may make it easier to go on, and may make it easier for the composer who can generate that sense of determinate *'Verbindlichkeit'* to get work performed, and gain recognition, to influence others, etc. but it still may be in some sense an illusion.[26] This might be connected with some of the remarks Adorno makes about the *'Entlastungseffekt'* of certain formal procedures.[27]

The view Adorno expresses at *GS* 16.537f. about increased subjective freedom arising out of *'Materialbeherrschung'* seems to be oddly utopian in a negative sense, namely it would be nice if it were true, but we really have no reason to expect it to be true – it arises *'aus dem Bedürfnis, nicht aus der Natur der Sache'* (*GS* 16.498).[28]

Finally, and this brings me to my third point, I wonder whether the tract really *works* as an avant-garde manifesto. Are its formulations really illuminating and appropriately directive? What would it be for a work of philosophy to be 'appropriately' directive in this area? It is, by the way, a repeated failing of traditional dialectics to confuse giving a description of what *would* have to be shown for a certain dichotomy to be overcome or for a certain problem to be solved with actually solving the problem, and I wonder if Adorno doesn't fall into this traditional trap. The idea of *'musique informelle'* seems to me to vacillate uninformatively between the banal and the utopian. Either the idea is just that music should not be subjected to abstract, pre-given forms *taken from outside* and imposed on it. It should be autonomous, giving itself its own law, and thus subjecting any forms it might use to creative transformation. This is fair enough, but is not really news. Or it is the idea of a music that literally was *without form*. Actually there seem to be at least three different possible theses here, running, from weakest to strongest: a) music in the future should dispense with *formulae*, i.e. untransformed repetition of clichés; b) music should dispense with *traditional* categories not just *formulae* and develop *new* categories (but categories that would have something like the same cognitive standing as the old categories had, i.e. would in principle be usable potentially to analyze a number of different works, and could presumably be used to compose other works); c) music should dispense with detachable categories altogether and aspire to a comprehensibility and coherence that is strictly internal, and can't be grasped in any external general concepts, a music which fully realized a certain ideal of musical 'nominalism' (*GS* 16.502) in which each work was a unique individual, uniquely only itself, one whose internal constitution, although inherently comprehensible, was not even potentially subsumable in any aesthetically interesting way under any series of possible categories that would classify it as 'the same' as some other work. It would, of course, be difficult to see how one could speak of the 'necessity' (*GS* 16.619) of a sequence, if it really was as unrepeatably unique as this variant suggests. This third variant would be compatible with it being possible to subsume the work under some 'external' (i.e. aesthetically insignificant) categories such as 'piece for solo piano', 'piece employing electronically generated sounds', etc. just as one could categorize abstract paintings as 'oil painting', 'collage', etc. The point is not that the work as a whole is or is not categorizable *at all*, but that it cannot be broken down into aesthetically significant constituent elements that instantiate categories; the work is constructed, as Max Paddison has suggested,[29] in such a way as to resist assimilation to the familiar through *internal* structural negation of traditional categories. One complication is that many of the traditional ways of categorizing pieces of music look 'external' but actually aren't. Thus to speak of something as a 'symphony' may not be thought to indicate with great precision what internal structure it will exhibit (because part of the effect may be to disappoint or thwart such expectations) but it will probably indicate a space of possible aesthetic expectations within which the work is located.[30] *'Musique informelle'* in this third sense would be music that went beyond itself and became something like painting.[31] As Adorno puts it in *'Vers une musique informelle'* (*GS* 16.517): *'Die bis zum Nullpunkt gelockerte Notation visiert eine Musik, die allen Erntes gänzlich so würde, wie sie es sonst nur verspricht'*. That is, every work of art is tacitly committed to striving to be a good work. To be such a good work means to try to be unique, new, etc., but that would mean not even to be notatable (i.e. *'notierbar'*), because anything notatable will by that fact alone exhibit subjugation to traditional categories, i.e. failure to be radically 'new'. This sounds like a paradox in the pejorative sense of that term, a tricky verbal manoeuvre that purports to prove something that couldn't possibly be true (such as Zeno's paradoxes, or the paradox about the impossibility of learning at the beginning of *'Meno'*) and which derives its plausibility from some deep-seated but virtually invisible error.

One corollary of Adorno's view would seem to be that genuinely successful music would not be analysable. Fortunately for analysis, Adorno also thinks that success in that sense is also impossible – it is a *utopian* condition to which music aspires but which it is fated, for more than empirical reasons, never to reach – and in the non-utopian conditions of the modern world analysis becomes more rather than less necessary than it was in times past, because music, in striving to become radically new does so by a more and more complex and potentially esoteric series of transformations of the old and well-known, and each such transformation can be analysed (and in fact must be analysed if the music and its significant form are to be comprehended).

III

I'm very struck by the *disanalogy* here between Adorno's views about philosophy and his views about the possibilities of (new) music. Thus at *GS* 16.533 he is discussing the notion of a *'musique informelle'* specifically, I take it, in its difference from traditional thematic-motivic music, serialism or aleatory forms of music and claims *'Der Verlauf [einer solchen 'musique informelle' – RG.] aber muß leisten, was einmal thematische Arbeit leistete, auch wenn auf all deren Mittel, auf Identität, Variation, Oberflächenzusammenhang der Motivik, erbarmunglos verzichtet wird'*. Now this seems to suggest a possibility for music which is one language (and philosophy as dependent on language) does not have. That is, it at least strongly suggests that music could give up the whole traditional apparatus of definition of identity, difference, etc. and yet reconstitute some kind of coherence. This is something he seems to me quite clearly to reject as a possibility for conceptual thought. At least in the realm of thought and cognition Adorno always emphasises that we really have no alternative to conceptual thought, even though we may know that it is in some sense implicated in an instrumental attempt to control nature about which it is appropriate to have serious reservations.[32] We can't start from any kind of immediate preconceptual experience or from a *tabula rasa* but always must begin from the given apparatus and set of concepts. The best 'thought' can do is work *within* the existing framework of concepts, rules, criteria, names and break it down internally, tacking back and forth between the general/universal and the particular. It can't either break out or revolutionize the framework itself.

This difference might be connected with the obvious difference in the role conceptual thought and art respectively play in the process of *'Selbsterhaltung'*. We don't perhaps *need* art to survive in quite the same way in which we need simple forms of conceptual thought (and then eventually science). It is the need for *'Selbsterhaltung'*, Adorno claims, that gives rise to our need for mastery of nature (*'Naturbeherrschung'*) and thus to the categorial scheme we use to give us cognition of the world. Adorno notoriously thought that reality was *so* dangerous that *no* amount of *Angst* about it was too much (*'Vor der Welt so wie sie ist, kann man gar nicht zuviel Angst haben'*). The Enlightenment as a form of obsession with rules is a natural (if paranoid) response to the real state of the world[33] and, Adorno thinks, it thus creates a world in which it is even more natural and rational to be paranoid. Rules are an attempt to introduce order, predictability, and security into an uncertain and threatening world. Art is perhaps sufficiently far from the primary demands of *'Selbsterhaltung'* that it can perhaps dissociate itself completely from *'die sture Komplizität . . . mit der Naturbeherrschung'* (*GS* 16.534) which is embedded in its traditional set of forms. *'Das Schlechte ist das Sekuritätsbedürfnis als solches'* (*GS* 16.524). Probably we can't give this need for security up in reality and live 'without *angst*',[34] but art is, or at any rate could perhaps be, a (possibly utopian) 'place', a 'no-where', where one could drop one's defenses and the associated obsession with order, rules, predictability, etc. and allow oneself to be surprised, etc. (*GS* 16.513ff). *'Musique informelle'* would be the expression of that utopian freedom. If one accepts Adorno's view that the resistance to 'new' music is a psychological reaction of those with weak egos who feel threatened by too much freedom, then ability to compose (and appreciate) *'musique informelle'* would be a sign of psychic health, freedom and ego-strength.[35]

IV

Adorno's image of the new as like the child sitting at the piano looking for a chord that has never been heard before (*ÄT* 55) is a poor model. The chord *was* already there (and, once found, will be capable of analysis). We think that if we are, for instance, trying to measure some natural magnitude of an object in the world – its length or weight – the answer is *there* waiting to be found even before we find it, and sculptors have occasionally claimed that the finished statue was 'already there in' the block of material, just waiting for some external roughness to be chipped off to reveal it, but we don't usually think of paintings as 'already there' before they have been executed, and we certainly don't think of a Beckett novel, to take the example of one of Adorno's favourite contemporary authors, as waiting out there (in French or English?) to be revealed by the typewriter. Note that although we might say of a specific chord on a 'tempered' piano that it is 'out there waiting' to be found, we are less tempted to speak of a whole composition employing that chord as 'out there'. I take it that part of the point Adorno is trying to make with this metaphor is one *against* electronic music: Just because one can produce sounds that are not found on the keyboard of a traditional tempered piano, one shouldn't *automatically* assume that one has entered the realm of the 'new' or created anything genuinely 'new'. That may well be perfectly true, but still not relevant. It may be that novelty of the sounds of which a piece is composed is not sufficient to guarantee the originality of the piece without it being the case that 'the new' is appropriately conceived as finding an as yet unknown combination on a pre-existing range of possibilities.

Adorno's usage of 'the new' seems to encompass a) the different, i.e. what is just 'other than' what went before', b) the 'original' or 'creative' in some aesthetically positive sense (so that not everything that was 'different' would necessarily be 'original' because the difference might just be of an aesthetically irrelevant kind), and finally c) the *'imprévu'* in two slightly different senses, namely first that which comes upon the listener with the shock of unexpectedness, as when the *Tristan*-chord occurs in the final movement of Berg's *Lyric Suite*, or second that which was not predicted or planned by the composer. Obviously *'l'imprévu'* in those two senses won't coincide because we know, for instance, that Berg planned and

worked long and hard to get the *Tristan*-chord into the composition at that point in a way that would strike the listener as
*'imprévu'*. Finally at the end of *'Vers une musique informelle'*
Adorno speaks of the aspiration the artist should have to create
things of which we don't know what they are (*GS* 16.540:
*'Dinge machen von denen wir nicht wissen, was sie sind'*). Of course,
to say that 'we don't know what they are' must be understood
subject to the qualifications given above (p. 155f.). This seems a
fifth sense of 'the new'. It also seems a much more plausible
image of 'the new' than that of the child at the piano. I note also
that this way of thinking would represent a step in the direction
of Kant (*KdU* §§ 46–49) for whom the talent for fine art was
the ability to create *'ästhetische Ideen'*, sensible representations
that resisted reduction to concepts.[36]

The fact that music utterly without form is probably impossible is not, I think, an objection, or at any rate I am not putting it
as an objection. Rather what I want to ask is: Did (and does)
this idea of a music without form really give composers a way
of putting (roughly) Boulez and Cage together, or finding a
third way forward? I've been concerned in this essay with what
I take to be attempts to think in an inappropriately or excessively deterministic way about the history of music and composition, and I've strongly suggested that a tendency in this
direction might result from a confusion of retrospective accounts, analysing a given successful composition or kind of
composing, and 'prospective' accounts.

Adorno at one point criticizes 'positivists' for always taking
everything too literally and perhaps he would have included
what I called above 'taking the dialectic seriously' (*supra* p.
154ff.) in this condemnation. Max Paddison has pointed out[37]
that Adorno held that 'in psychoanalysis only the exaggerations are true',[38] and has suggested that perhaps Adorno's own
views are to be taken as exaggerations or metaphors. That
might be one way of proceeding. When Adorno speaks of a
'convergence' of art and philosophy (*ÄT* 197), the 'converging'

is not presumably intended to be all from one side of the dichotomy. If 'genuine aesthetic experience must become philosophical or it won't exist' (*ÄT* 197), then presumably philosophy
must also become 'aesthetic' and perhaps the appropriate form
of this is the use of metaphors, fictive constructions, and hyper-
bole. Adorno certainly was in favour of overcoming the distinction between literal truth and 'artistic truth' as much as possible, and perhaps he thought that modern music was amenable
to understanding only through an analysis that was itself a kind
of work of art, employing metaphors and using concepts such
as 'truth', 'necessity', *'Zwang'*, etc. in exaggerated or non-literal
ways. Metaphors, of course, don't interpret themselves and it
would be important to know when, in what contexts, and to
what extent a given metaphorical or non-literal usage was useful and when not. One may wonder in general about the relation of forms of understanding (especially the highly developed
kind of formal analysis which it is one of the glories of music to
permit) to forms of new production.

What, finally, do composers *want* from philosophers? Is what
Adorno gives what they want (and need)? Perhaps it is a mistake to think there is any particular thing they *need* and perhaps
they will be grateful for any number of different things they
might get. Creativity is notoriously an idiosyncratic phenomenon and flourishes under what seem sometimes to be bizarre
circumstances. Lots of things can be highly stimulating without
being 'true'. Numerological fantasies, reading Mallarmé, transcendental meditation, mycology, etc. may well have shown
themselves in one context or other to be 'useful' in stimulating
the productive imagination. Adorno seems to have thought
that, at any rate in the second half of the twentieth century,
theoretical cognition – not just ability to do musical analysis, but
also in some sense 'philosophical' cognition – was a virtually
indispensible component of compositional ability, and I suspect
he hoped that his own work would provide the 'cognition'
needed. Does it do that or is it really more like numerology?

NOTES

1 This paper was originally a series of comments I made as respondent
to a Roundtable Discussion on 'The concept of form in the new
music' at a conference on *'The category of the "new": Adorno, analysis,*
*and contemporary composition'* sponsored by the Society for Music
Analysis and held at Goldsmiths College in London on 21 February
1998. I'm very grateful to the four main speakers at the Roundtable:
Brian Ferneyhough (University of California at San Diego), Claus-
Steffan Mahnkopf (Freiburg/Br.), David Osmond-Smith (Sussex),
and Roger Redgate (Goldsmiths); to Max Paddison (Durham) who
invited me to participate and chaired the session; finally to the three
other main speakers at the conference, Robert Adlington (Sussex),
Julian Johnson (Sussex), and Alastair Williams (Keele). I'm also
grateful to Hilary Gaskin, Istvan Hont, Max Paddison, and Quentin
Skinner for reading and commenting on drafts of this essay.

2 Cf. *Klassik, Romantik, neue Musik; GS* 16.126ff.

3 For a different reading, cf. Max Paddison, *Adorno's aesthetics of music*
(CUP, 1993), esp. chapter 6. Paddison analyses Adorno's view of the
history of music with great subtlety as a dialectic of continuities *and*
discontinuities.

4 Cf. Schönberg's famous statement about *'die Emanzipation der*
*Dissonanz'* in *'Komposition mit zwölf Tönen'* (*Stil und Gedanke*, S.74).

5 Cf. his *Art* (London, 1914).

6 Cf. *ÄT* 193–205.

7 For a good account of some of the issues that arise here, cf. Max
Paddison 'Adorno's Aesthetics of Modernism' in his *Adorno, modern-*
*ism and mass culture: Essays on Critical Theory and music* (Kahn &
Averill, London, 1996), pp. 45ff.

8 Obviously this question, which has to do with artistic *'form'*, is
distinct from the question about the way in which language-use
which obeys pre-existing rules can transmit *new* information.

9 One might compare this with Lessing's famous comment (discussed
at great length at the beginning of Kierkegaard's *Concluding Unscien-*
*tific Postscript*): *'Wenn Gott in seiner Rechten alle Wahrheit, und in seiner*
*Linken den einzigen immer regen Trieb nach Wahrheit, obschon mit dem*
*Zusatz mich immer und ewig zu irren, verschlossen hielte, und spräche zu*
*mir: wähle! Ich fiele ihm in Demut in seine Linke und sagte: Vater, gieb! die*
*reine Wahrheit ist ja doch nur für dich allein.'*

10 Cf. *'Das Altern der neuen Musik'* in Adorno's collection *Dissonanzen*
(Vandenhoek & Ruprecht, 1963), pp. 136ff.

11 Oddly enough, although Adorno in general tries to detach art as much as possible from intrinsic connection with happiness (*'Glück'*; cf. *ÄT* 30), he repeatedly speaks of the happiness that accompanies thought, understanding, and cognition (e.g. at *GS* 16.495 where he speaks of *'das bittere Glück des Denkens'*).

12 Although Schönberg seems to have thought that a piece of music expressed what he called a *'Gedanke'* (cf. *Stil und Gedanke*, p. 32ff.). Hegel, *Werke* 7.26: *'die Eitelkeit des Besserwissens'*.

13 Plato, *Apology* 21b–23a. Obviously Socrates' and Plato's use of 'dialectic' is not the same as Hegel's.

14 Many of the actual dialectical transitions one finds in Hegel's work quite clearly have this property – there is no way in which anyone who was standing in the grip of the contradiction could by cognitive analysis work his way out to the resolution; as Hegel says in the *'Vorrede'* to *PhG*, something must *happen*, spirit must *work* to get to the next step, and only once it has reached the next step can it look back and see that the motion it instantiated exhibited a logical structure.

15 Cf. Sophocles, *Antigone* ll. 450ff.

16 Schönberg, as is well-known, disapproved of this term, but I will use it assuming readers know what I mean.

17 Hegel, *Werke* 7.28.

18 *'Ismen'* are the aesthetic equivalents of *'Standpunkte'* and *'Standpunkte'* are notoriously incompatible, in Hegel's view, with speculative philosophy. Cf. Hegel, *Werke* (Suhrkamp), vol. 3. pp. 11f.; Adorno, *Negative Dialektik* (Suhrkamp, 1966), pp. 14ff. Cf. also *ÄT* 43f.

19 Cf. *Minima Moralia* (Suhrkamp, 1951), §32.

20 For the best discussion of the concept of the musical 'material' cf. Max Paddison's *Adorno's aesthetics of music* (CUP, 1993), and also the essays collected in his *Adorno, modernism, and mass culture: Essays on Critical Theory and music* (Kahn & Averill, London, 1996).

21 Cf. *ÄT* 182–193. Adorno, of course, would *really* like to have it both ways: art is a riddle which both does and doesn't have a solution, is both determinate and indeterminate. It isn't as if this view is obviously subject to serious objections, but it also doesn't seem very helpful.

22 Note that this distinction mirrors another distinction, namely that between thinking of what a composer is doing as creating a new *style* or *way* of composing (e.g. 'method of composing with twelve tones related only to each other') and thinking of a composer as

producing a particular individual work. If one thinks of this the first way, then it is tempting to think of *'material'* in the *geschichts-philosophisch* sense; if one thinks in the second way, then it is tempting to use the phenomenological sense.

23  *ÄT 222, 'Material . . . ist, womit die Künstler schalten . . . alles ihnen Gegenübertretende, worüber sie zu entscheiden haben.'*

24  *'Form in der neuen Musik'* in *GS* 16.626.

25  *'Form in der neuen Musik'* in *GS* 16.619.

26  Brian Ferneyhough in his contribution to the Roundtable made a remark to the effect that a composer today who recognized how difficult it is to change the Self might try to deal with this by attempting to propel that Self into the Other. I'm struck in general by the absence of the term 'expression' from the normal vocabu-lary of contemporary composers – that would mean that Adorno is right in claiming that the 'ideal of expression' had been irreversibly superseded (*GS* 16.502) – and by the potential usefulness of Adorno's metaphor of *'Reibungskoeffizient'* (*GS* 16.499) for the phe-nomenon Ferneyhough describes. I take it, though, that Ferney-hough sees so much in Adorno because his own compositional practice is in a sense the exact mirror image of that Adorno describes – there is nothing so much like the left hand as the right (although they can't be brought to coincide). When Adorno speaks of *'Residuen [die] die integrale Durchbildung des Phänomens wie Fremdkörper stören'* (*GS* 16.496), he is speaking of something to be avoided. Ferneyhough's integration of chaotic elements – not, per-haps *'Residuen'* but clearly *'Fremdkörper'* and *meant to be perceived* as *'Fremdkörper'* – is such an attempt productively to propel the Self out to its Other. The question is whether an illusory 'other' – if the conception that the material makes determinate demands is an illusion – can serve the appropriate function.

27  *GS* 16.505.

28  Isn't it actually much the same as the excessively optimistic view by Eimert which Adorno criticizes at *GS* 16.509?

29  Private communication.

30  Max Paddison in his Introduction to the Roundtable cited as a metaphor of what Adorno might have meant by *'musique infor-melle'* a passage from Beckett (Adorno's favourite contemporary writer) in which a figure takes an inventory of objects in his pocket. Among these is an object the figure cannot categorize. Paddison suggests that this object is one later found and described as a 'knife-rest'. This suggests, quite correctly, that to say the object

isn't 'categorizable' doesn't mean that one can't give lots of correct general descriptions of it, but that one doesn't know what the object is *for* (and finally sees, if Paddison is right in connecting the two passages in question, that it is *for* resting a knife on). This looks to me like a parody of Kant's doctrine of aesthetic beauty as *'Zweckmäßigkeit ohne Zweck'* (Kant, *KdU* §17) – the object must be beautiful because it looks as if it must be *for* something, but one can't tell what it is for – but, as is so often the case in Beckett, it is a parody which makes a serious philosophical point. The very uselessness, the non-fungibility, of art in the contemporary world is for Adorno an important part of the way in which it exercises its critical vocation (*ÄT* 203, 335ff). This is slightly different from the demand that the *internal* structure of a work of music exhibit nothing that could be grasped in categories that had potentially multiple instances.

31  Cf. Nelson Goodman, *Languages of Art,* chapter IV (Bobbs-Merrill, Indianapolis and New York, 1968).

32  E.g. *Negative Dialektik* (Suhrkamp, 1966), p. 24 *et passim.*

33  Adorno and Horkheimer, *Dialektik der Aufklärung* (Fischer, 1969), p. 22.

34  Cf. Adorno, *Minima Moralia* §§66,128; *Negative Dialektik,* p. 94.

35  Adorno believes that fear of what is 'other' or 'different' (and thus *a fortiori* of any novelty) is a deep-seated and invariant feature of human life (cf. *Dialektik der Aufklärung*). Late capitalism, however, is qualitatively much more powerful and all-encompassing than any previous form of socio-economic organization; it is able actually to make the natural and the human world uniform. In late-capitalist societies it is, therefore, especially difficult for individuals to develop the specific abilities needed to respond adequately to new music.

36  In his paper 'Adorno and Musical Temporality' (presented at the Goldsmiths Conference) Robert Adlington drew attention to the importance of tonal ambiguity in many strands of contemporary music. He connected this with the possibility of escaping from some of the difficulties Adorno finds in traditional concepts of musical temporality. It seems to me that the phenomenon of tonal ambiguity might also allow a certain rehabilitation of *'Schein'* as a category in modern music, a suspicion that was reinforced by some of Brian Ferneyhough's comments about the ways in which objects and processes can shadow each other in his work, and about ways in which structures can be seen as belonging to various

archeological strata, depending partly on the history of their derivation.

37 In the Roundtable Discussion at Goldsmiths College.
38 Adorno, *Minima Moralia* § 29, cf. §§ 82,128; Cf. *Eingriffe* (Suhrkamp, 1963), p. 152.

# 7

## NIETZSCHE AND MORALITY

ALTHOUGH he occasionally referred to himself as an 'im-moralist' (EH *'Warum ich ein Schicksal bin'*), in one impor-tant sense Nietzsche was not one, if only because he didn't in fact think that there was a single, distinct phenomenon – 'morality' – which it would make much sense to be universally in favour of or opposed to. Nietzsche was a conscious anti-essentialist in that he didn't think that terms like 'morality' always and everywhere referred to items that shared the same defining traits. Rather he had a view like that which Wittgen-stein was to develop fifty or sixty years later: There isn't any 'essence of morality' (or 'of religion' or 'of truth' or what-not), that is any set of important properties that all instances of what can correctly be called 'morality' must exhibit. 'Morality' en-compasses a wide variety of different sorts of things that are at best connected to each other by 'family resemblances', and there are no antecedently specifiable limits to what can count as sufficient 'resemblance' to make the term 'morality' cor-rectly applicable.

Thus I take the point of the third essay in JGB, entitled *'Das religiöse Wesen'* to be precisely that there isn't any such thing as 'the essence' of religion. There are just different constellations of practices, beliefs, and institutions that have very different origins, internal structures, motivational properties, and social functions, each constellation having 'sufficient' similarity to some other constellations to allow the same word ('religion') to be used of all of them, but what counts as 'sufficient' similarity is antecedently indeterminate, and no two religions will necessarily be at all 'similar' in any given significant respect. Another way of putting this is that for Nietzsche there is no absolutely clear and sharp distinction between literal and metaphorical usage or between the proper and an extended sense of a term (cf. ÜWL).

Anti-essentialism, properly understood, need not imply that one can say nothing general and true about all the instances that happen to be taken to fall under a certain term. That the members of a family resemble each other not by virtue of all having the same essential feature (e.g. the same kind of nose or lip) but by virtue of different similarities individuals have in different features, does not mean that there is nothing true that can be said about all members of the family, for instance that they all are human beings, or all have noses (of one sort or another, if that is true of them). That, in turn, needn't imply that we couldn't call a cat or horse an important member of the family, or for that matter that we couldn't in some contexts properly call an old violin, a portrait, or a glass a member of the family.

There are, then, an indefinite number of different (possible and actual) kinds of things that could be called 'morality' without impropriety (JGB §186). Some of these different moralities exist at different times and places, but some may overlap. 'Modern' people (i.e. late nineteenth-century middle-class Central Europeans) are best understood not as bearers of a single unitary *Sittlichkeit*[1] but rather as standing under the influence of a variety of diverse forms of morality (JGB §215). In fact, Nietzsche holds that it is a sign of an especially elevated spiritual life to experience in oneself the unresolved struggle of incompatible moral points of view and forms of evaluation (GM I. 16). Just because there are so many different types of morality, it makes sense, Nietzsche thinks, to begin the study of morality with a natural history of the phenomenon, a 'typology' of the existing forms of morality, and an investigation of their origins, functions, relative strengths, and characteristic weaknesses (JGB §186ff.).

Despite the wide variability of what could legitimately be called 'morality', in nineteenth-century Europe 'morality' had come to be used most commonly to designate one particular form of morality, important parts of which were ultimately derived from Christianity. The claim that there was a dominant morality in nineteenth-century Europe which developed out of Christianity is not incompatible with the claim made at JGB §215 and cited above that 'modern' people characteristically live according to a variety of different moralities. First of all the specifically Christian morality may have been predominant in the recent past (i.e. up to the beginning of the nineteenth century) and may have just recently (as of the middle of the nineteenth century) begun to be displaced by other forms of morality, but this process may be incomplete. Second, Christian morality may have been and to some extent may still be 'dominant' in the sense that it governs wide areas of life (although perhaps not all areas), has a kind of public and quasi-official standing and defines the terms in which people think and speak about morality when they are thinking most reflectively or speaking in a public context. This might be true even though in other areas of life people also use other standards of evaluation, have other forms of sensibility, etc. which are incompatible with the Christian ones. They may fail to be aware that their sensibility and their reactions are not fully and exclusively Christian, they may assess actions by standards that diverge from those of Christianity and have a slightly guilty conscience about this, they may explicitly assess individual actions in concrete cases by non-Christian standards, but remain under the influence of Christianity when it comes to giving general theoretical form to their reflections on morality, etc.

Given Nietzsche's location in history and his anti-essentialism, it is not odd for him sometimes to follow widespread usage and use 'morality' to refer to the specifically Christian (or immediately post-Christian) morality of the European nineteenth century. In reading Nietzsche it is thus very important to try to determine in each particular case whether he is using 'morality' in the narrow sense to mean (nineteenth-century Christian) morality or in a more general sense.

Nietzsche specifically states that the fact that there are many different 'moralities' should *not* be interpreted to mean that no form of morality is at all binding (*'verbindlich'* FW §345). Given his general position, one would also expect him to think that there are very different kinds of 'bindingness'. The Christian conscience and the Kantian specifically moral 'ought' are not universal phenomena, but the historical products of particular circumstances. They don't have the universal, unconditional validity claimed for them by Kantians and Christians, but it doesn't follow from that that they don't have some other kind of *'Verbindlichkeit'* at least for some people in some circumstances. Furthermore, Nietzsche repeatedly stresses that valuation, giving preference to one thing over another, discrimination is a central part of the way we live as human beings (GM II. 8); he sometimes even calls it a fundamental property of 'life itself' (JGB §9).[2]

II

These preliminary remarks suggest that although Nietzsche is against the dominant nineteenth-century form of morality, he isn't necessarily against morality *tout court*. To place oneself beyond good and evil need not mean to place oneself beyond good and bad or to become indifferent to discriminations between good and less good (GM I. 17). If one thinks of a morality, for instance, just as a non-random way of discriminating good from less good, it isn't clear how it could make much sense to be against that. If one takes the passage at FW §345 seriously, Nietzsche seems to be claiming that there could be systematic forms of evaluation or discrimination that did have a hold on us, one or another kind of *'Verbindlichkeit'* for us (although not, of course, a *'Verbindlichkeit'* of the kind claimed by traditional Christian morality). Such binding forms of valuation might be thought to be potentially the kernel of the 'higher form of morality' which Nietzsche sometimes suggests is possible (JGB §202) and which, whatever other properties it might have, would not be subject to the kinds of criticism Nietzsche levels against Christian morality.

Whether or not the above is a plausible line of thought may become clearer if one first examines the exact nature of Nietzsche's objections to Christian morality and its derivatives.

Nietzsche holds that the traditional European morality derived from Christianity is structured by six characteristic theses:

(1) This morality claims of itself that it is 'unconditional' in the obligations it imposes. (JGB §199)
(2) It claims a kind of universality, i.e. to apply equally to all human beings. (JGB §§198, 221)
(3) It claims that only free human actions have moral value. (JGB §32; GM I. 13)
(4) It claims that the moral worth of a free action depends on the quality of the human choice that leads the agent to perform it. (JGB §32)
(5) It claims that human beings and their actions are to be evaluated (positively) as 'good' or (negatively) as 'evil' depending on the kind of human choice involved. (JGB §260)
(6) It claims that we are responsible for our choices and should feel guilt or remorse for evil choices, etc. (GM I. 13, III.15, 20)[3]

Nietzsche wishes to claim (contra (1) above) that 'the taste for the unconditional is the worst of all tastes' (JGB §31). Slaves are the kind of people who need and keenly desire the unconditional or absolute because they really understand only tyranny (JGB §46, cf. §§198, 199, 221). I take Nietzsche's argument here to be something like the following: The plausibility of (1) results from a kind of fascination with the idea of unconditional obligations, but the most plausible explanation for this fascination is that it arises out of an extreme need for order and predictability which is a frequently encountered trait of weak and helpless people who face a potentially dangerous and unstable environment, and who are understandably ready to grasp at virtually any means to introduce regularity into their world. An 'unconditional obligation' is one that could be counted on no matter what and hence one that would introduce a high degree of predictability into at least some portion of the world. People who are especially strong or competent in a particular domain or respect, Nietzsche thinks, don't need to fear the lack of absolute, unconditional predictability in that domain – if they are truly strong and competent, they will expect to be able to deal with whatever comes up, even with the unpredictable and unexpected. If one adds to this account that slaves in addition to being weak (as Nietzsche assumes) will also be likely to have as their basic direct experience of the social order the absolute commands given to them by their masters, it wouldn't be surprising if slaves developed the 'bad taste' of a fascination with unconditional obligation. So Nietzsche wishes to reverse what he takes to have been the traditional prejudice: To keep looking for the absolute, the unconditional, the 'essential' (which is just the set of properties a thing can absolutely reliably be expected to have) is not a sign of special superiority or profundity, but of a servile disposition too weak to tolerate disorder, complexity, ambiguity, and the unpredictable (cf. JGB §59 and FW §5).

The above isn't, of course, an argument against the existence of unconditional obligations, but then Nietzsche thinks it is as much of an argument against them as any argument that has been given for them. Given the kind of thesis this is, psychological considerations about the type of person who is most likely to find this approach to morality plausible are, Nietzsche believes, perfectly appropriate. It is no argument against Nietzsche's view here to claim that it is in some sense necessary or highly desirable for us to introduce order and predictability into our social world by assigning unconditional obligations to one another because otherwise things would be too chaotic for human life to continue. Whether or not this is true, it is not incompatible with the Nietzschean view I have just described. All humans may just be so weak that we need this kind of order. In the first instance Nietzsche merely wishes to claim a connection between the need for order (which lies, he thinks, behind the ascription of absolute obligations) and the relative level of strength and weakness of those who feel the need to ascribe such obligations. It is a completely separate issue whether or not some person or people might be so strong as to be able to dispense with the very idea of an unconditional obligation altogether.

Nietzsche goes so far in rejecting the universality of morality as to assert at one point that it is 'immoral' (*'unmoralisch'*) to hold that the same moral code should apply to all (JGB §221, cf. JGB 43, 46, 198, 199, 228, 284). To the extent to which he gives reasons for this rejection which go beyond appeals to 'taste' (JGB §43)[4] these reasons seem to depend on his doctrines of 'rank-ordering' and of the 'pathos of distance'. Nietzsche believes that in general[5] the creation of positive values, the 'elevation of the human type' (JGB §257), can result only from what he calls the 'pathos of distance' (JGB §257, GM I. 2). The 'pathos of distance' is the long-lasting feeling on the part of a 'higher ruling order' of its total superiority in relation to a 'lower' order, and although this feeling may eventually take a more sublimated form, its origin will be in crude relations of physical domination of one group over another, that is, in some form of slavery (GS). Only such a 'distance' between 'rank-orders' generates the requisite tension, as it were, to allow new

173

values to be created. So originally slavery is not just instrumentally necessary in order to provide (for instance) leisure for members of the upper classes to produce and appreciate various cultural artefacts, but rather slaves were a kind of social-psychological necessity because only if the members of a group have others to look down on and despise as wholly inferior will they be able to create positive values.[6] Valuing, Nietzsche thinks, is an inherently discriminatory activity; it is a positing of one thing as better than something else, and if this discrimination is to be active and positive it must arise out of the positive sense of self that can exist only in a society of 'rank-orders', i.e. where this kind of distance exists.[7]

Nietzsche's main objection to universal forms of morality is that they tend to break down the rank-ordering in society. In a rank-ordered society there will be different codes governing behaviour among members of the same rank and behaviour of the members of one rank to those of another (JGB §260). If the rank-ordering of a society is undermined, the pathos of distance will be in danger of disappearing and the society will run the risk of losing the ability to produce new positive values (JGB §202). A society unable to produce new positive values is decadent, and Nietzsche seems to think such decadence is self-evidently the worst thing that can happen to a society. This line of argument presupposes that one can give a relatively clear sense to the distinction between active, positive valuation and negative, reactive valuation, and that the 'health' which consists in the continued ability to produce new positive values is the most appropriate final framework for discussing forms of morality. So theses (1) and (2) are to be rejected.

Notoriously Nietzsche denies that there is any such thing as 'free will' (JGB §21; GD *'Die vier großen Irrtümer'* §7). His denial that the will is free doesn't imply that he thinks the will is unfree, enslaved, or in bondage. Rather he holds that the whole conceptual pair 'free/unfree' is a fiction having no real application to 'the will'.[8] 'Free will' was an invention of weak

people (slaves) who appropriated a certain contingently existing grammatical distinction to be found in Indo-European languages, the distinction between the grammatical subject of a
sentence and its predicate, and transposed this distinction into
the realm of metaphysics (JGB §17; GM I. 13; GD *'Die "Vernunft" in der Philosophie'* §5). Just as the grammatical subject
can be distinguished from the grammatical predicate, so also,
they claimed, there stands an entity (the subject, agent, self,
ego) *behind* every activity. Just as one can affirm or deny that
the predicate applies to the subject, the subject remaining the
while the same (*'ambulat Caius'/'non ambulat Caius'*), so similarly the I or self or ego stands separate from and indifferent to
possible actions, so that it is a genuinely open question whether
it will perform a certain action or not. That it is purportedly
such an open question means, for the slave, that the agent has
free will. The slaves then proceed to connect forms of moral
evaluation with the correct or incorrect use of 'free will'.

Nietzsche thinks it is a mistake to believe that there is a
separate 'agent' standing apart from and behind action. All
there is is the activity itself. There isn't any 'it' that rains or
thunders, just raining and thundering. An activity can be more
or less forceful, a human being more or less powerful, even (to
stretch language a bit) a will 'stronger' or 'weaker' (JGB §21),
but none of this implies that people have 'free choice' to be or
not be what and who they are and to act accordingly.

With the invention of 'free will' the slaves pursue two related goals at once. First of all the fiction of free will allows
them to aggrandize themselves falsely by turning their real
weakness into grounds for self-congratulation. In fact they are
not aggressive or successful because they are weak, but they
now have the resources to give an account of this deficiency as
morally meritorious. Instead of feeling weak – realizing that
they can't do certain things – they feel morally superior (and
thus in some sense 'strong') because they falsely believe that
they could have done various things which they actually didn't

do, but never did because they meritoriously *chose* never to do them. The second goal is that of confounding and debilitating the strong as much as possible. If the slaves can succeed in lodging their fictitious notion of 'free will' (with some of its associated baggage) in the minds of those who are stronger, they will have improved the conditions of their life considerably. To the extent to which the strong come to think of themselves as having 'free will' they will in fact begin to have a tendency to separate themselves from their actions and this will tend to make them less powerfully and spontaneously active than before, a situation advantageous to the slaves (GM I. 13).

Given this account of 'free will' Nietzsche believes he can reject theses (3) and (4) out of hand, and, since the distinction between 'good' and 'evil' depends on the slaves' notion of 'free will' (GM I. 10, 11, 13), thesis (5) too.

'Guilt', 'remorse', (the sense of) 'sin' etc. are, Nietzsche believes, moralizing misinterpretations of underlying physiological conditions (GD *'Die "Verbesserer" der Menschheit'* §1). 'Guilt' arises originally as the expectation that I will suffer pain because of failure to discharge my debts (GM II. 4–8). Since cruelty, the pleasure of inflicting suffering on others, is, Nietzsche thinks, natural to humans (cf. JGB §229), and since justice requires that in commercial transactions equivalents be exchanged for equivalents,[9] it is also natural for a creditor whose debtor has defaulted to demand this in the form of a warrant to inflict that amount of pain on the debtor which will give the creditor pleasure equivalent to the pain the creditor incurred by the default. A strong empirical association of ideas thus gets established between failure to discharge obligations and the expectation of suffering pain. Furthermore, as Nietzsche believes, with urbanization people are forced to live in ever closer proximity to each other, and natural forms of aggression which primitive nomads could easily discharge outward without too much harm to themselves – and which in nomadic conditions might even be thought to be socially useful and thus rewarded – become inhibited (GM II. 16). In the narrow confines of the early cities more self-restraint becomes necessary. However, the aggression which is denied discharge outward doesn't just disappear. Rather people come to turn it against themselves in a variety of increasingly subtle ways (GM II. 16). They develop a need to vent their aggression on themselves, to make themselves suffer. It is also the case that in many societies at a certain point the relation between the individual and society as a whole comes to be reinterpreted as one of 'debt'. As an individual I am thought to receive certain valuable benefits 'from society' (e.g. protection) and what I owe in return is conformity to the customary morality (GM II. 9). The 'need-to-suffer' described above can then appropriate this notion of a 'debt to society'. I can learn to impose suffering on myself (in the form of 'bad conscience')[10] if I violate the customary morality.

The idea that a sense of guilt or remorse is a result of awareness that I am evil (because I have acted in an evil way) is a late, moralizing misinterpretation of this underlying physiological (or perhaps physio-psychological) condition which is really just a combination of fear and the need to direct aggression toward myself. Similarly in GM III. 16–20 Nietzsche has a lengthy and subtle account of the way in which 'sin' is a moralizing misinterpretation of various states of physical or psychological debility. That takes care of thesis (6).

III

There seem, then, to be two related kinds of objection Nietzsche has to the morality derived from Christianity:

1.  It is based on a series of particular mistakes and errors, especially on series of moralizing misinterpretations of natural or physiological facts.

177

2. It in general claims for itself the wrong kind of status, posits itself as absolute and universal.

At this point I would like to add a qualification to the previous discussion. At the start I spoke in a rather undifferentiated way about Nietzsche's 'rejection' of traditional morality, but it is actually part of Nietzsche's project to undercut as much as possible what he takes to be forms of naiveté that characterized traditional discussion in ethics, namely the assumption that a given view or form of morality had to be absolutely accepted (or rejected) once and for all for all times and places and for all people. 'Acceptance' or 'rejection' are for him much more context-dependent. The question in ethics is not: 'Is this the right way to act, live, feel, etc. for everyone, everywhere at all times?' but: 'What are the particular strengths and weaknesses of this form of morality for this person or this group of people at this time?'[11]

Nietzsche doesn't wish to 'blame' the proponents of the traditional Christian morality for being what they are, and developing the views, beliefs, habits, and attitudes they needed to make their way in the world (cf. GM III. 13). He points out, though, that many of these views are false and makes two predictions: a) it will become increasingly difficult for people in the modern world to avoid realizing that these beliefs are false, and b) that the dissolution of these beliefs will cause serious social and cultural dislocation. Supporters of traditional forms of morality may see in falsehood per se grounds for rejecting Christian morality wholesale, but that is an internal difficulty for traditional Christianity, committed as it is to a peculiar absolutist conception of Truth. Nietzsche states repeatedly and with all requisite explicitness that he has no objections to lies or illusions in themselves. Illusion, *Schein*, is necessary for life, and there would be no point in being 'against' it *simpliciter*. That Christian morality attempts to set itself absolutely against such *Schein* is another one of its limitations. Similarly it is a mistake for traditional morality to consider itself the *only,* exclusive, and universal morality, but *sometimes* a 'narrowing of horizons' may be one of the conditions of human growth and flourishing (JGB §188).

Even if Nietzsche does 'reject' the traditional morality for himself, it doesn't follow that he thinks its proponents must necessarily all reject it, too, or even that it would be a good idea for them all to give it up. Nietzsche may not think that he is himself bound by the canons of Christian morality, but whether or not it is a good idea for some others to hold themselves bound depends on what particular needs Christianity might serve for them, a topic about which much could be said in individual cases. Of course, Nietzsche by his writing has made it more difficult for a proponent of the traditional morality to hold fast to it (and to hold others to it), because he has focused attention on aspects of it that it will be difficult for traditional morality to acknowledge and deal with (for instance, the errors on which it is based), but that is a separate issue.

If Nietzsche does not, then, object to Christian morality because it is based on particular false beliefs or because it erroneously claims absolute status for itself, perhaps he objects to it because it is coercive, repressive, or tyrannical. He might have nothing against lying but have a rooted dislike of lies invented for the sake of justifying coercion. This would be a third possible line of objection.

Unfortunately Nietzsche also clearly has nothing against 'coercion' or 'tyranny' per se. They, too, can be conditions of growth (JGB §188). If Nietzsche's remarks about 'breeding' can be given any weight at all, they seem to indicate that under certain circumstances significant forms of coercion might even be highly desirable (cf. GM II. 1–2; JGB §262; GD *'Die "Verbesserer" der Menschheit'*). Finally there is Nietzsche's obvious admiration for the Platonic Lie, the resolute, honest lie told for the sake of imposing forms of social coercion (GM III. 19).

The passage at GM III. 19 in which Nietzsche contrasts the 'honest' lie of Plato with the 'dishonest' lying of Christianity suggests that perhaps 'honesty' is the crucial dimension. I take it that an 'honest' lie is a lie told by someone who knows clearly that it is an untruth and tells it ('resolutely') nonetheless. I tell a 'dishonest' lie when I am half deceiving myself while telling an untruth to another. A fourth possible version of Nietzsche's objection to Christian morality would then run:

4. Traditional morality is based on 'dishonest' lies (perhaps invented to justify repression and coercion).

Perhaps there is something especially disreputable about 'dishonest' lying, although it is hard to see how there can be anything especially wrong in half-deceiving myself, if there is nothing inherently wrong in (completely) deceiving others. Perhaps Nietzsche is opposed to 'dishonest' lying because he thinks it both a result of weakness and an obstacle to strength. I gain no *obvious* advantage from lying to myself of the kind I may gain from lying to others. So if I lie to myself I must have some reason. One plausible reason, Nietzsche thinks, is that I am too weak to face the truth (cf. JGB §39). One can also imagine various ways in which half-deceiving oneself might be thought to sap one's strength or make one less effective in dealing with others. This line of objection would then reduce to the claim that Christianity sapped human strength or vitality.

Another possible approach might start from the fact that Nietzsche describes Christian morality as a form of 'counter-nature' (*'Widernatur'*, cf. GD *'Moral als Widernatur'*). This might be connected with passages in which Nietzsche speaks of humanity as a 'plant' which must be made to grow and flourish. Some moralities (at some times and under some circumstances) contribute to the flourishing of this plant, while others stunt its growth (JGB §§44, 257f.). Nietzsche clearly has the hot-house rather than the lawn in mind when he uses this botanical imagery. The 'flourishing' of the plant 'humanity' does not consist in the survival of the maximal number of more or less homogeneous healthy blades, but in the production of a few individual human orchids, 'highest specimens' (cf. NNH §9; GM I. 16). These highest individual specimens are what arouse our admiration and their existence can even be said to 'justify' (*'rechtfertigen'*) humanity as a whole (GM I. 12).

So the fifth possible Nietzschean objection would run:

5. Traditional morality is contrary to nature in that it renders more difficult the emergence of the individual 'highest specimens' of humanity.

The operative part of this claim is the second part (i.e. what follows 'in that' above) because the term 'nature' is highly ambiguous and in at least some important senses of the term it is, for Nietzsche, no objection to say that something is 'contrary to nature'. Thus he writes (JGB §188): 'Every morality, in contrast to the policy of *laisser aller*, is a piece of tyranny against "nature", also against "reason": That, however, is no objection to the morality, unless one were to decree on the basis of some morality that all forms of tyranny and unreason were not allowed.'

If 'nature' doesn't provide a standard against which we can measure moralities, perhaps 'Life' does. In the new preface to the second edition of GT (*'Versuch einer Selbstkritik'* §4) Nietzsche claims that one of the major questions the work raises is: 'What is the significance of morality, viewed from the perspective of life (*unter der Optik des Lebens*)?' Perhaps the highest specimens are 'highest' because they exhibit a special vitality or represent Life at its most intense.

There is little doubt that 'Life' (and the self-affirmation of Life) in Nietzsche does seem to function as a criterion for evaluating moralities (GD *'Moral als Widernatur'* §5). Sometimes Nietzsche even speaks in a way that suggests that the course of human history is the story of life affirming itself in whatever way is possible under the given circumstances, for instance in his discussion of the 'priestly' revaluation of values which leads to the ascendency of a set of life-denying forms of valuation (GM III. 13). Paradoxically Nietzsche suggests here that this event can itself be seen as a way in which life is affirming itself. If 'Life' really does affirm itself in one way or the other, as best it can, under the given circumstances, and if those circumstances are in the given case those of a wholly debilitated population which is in danger of giving up on existence altogether – committing the kind of mass suicide Nietzsche thinks will be a very tempting option for such a population – the most vital form of willing possible might be willing to negate life in a focused structured way. This may be a very astute psychological observation about how best to deal with certain forms of social malaise. That isn't the issue here; rather the question is whether one can speak of 'Life' as an underlying form of meta-physical agency which *does* things. *Prima facie* this kind of appeal to 'Life' would seem to be incompatible with Nietzsche's general strictures on positing 'agents' that stand behind activities and also with one of the most interesting features of the discussion of history in Nietzsche's mature works, namely the denial that there is an underlying 'logic of history'. History, for Nietzsche, is just a sequence of contingent conjunctions, accidental encounters, and fortuitous collisions (GM II. 12–13), not the story of the unitary development or self-expression of some single underlying, non-empirical agency.

Contingency is such a striking property of much of history that it is perhaps not easy for us to see in what sense Nietzsche is not just stating the obvious. One well-known way of thinking about history in nineteenth-century Germany, however, saw the superficial contingency of individual events in history as fully compatible with the existence of an underlying logic of history. Thus for Hegel history is 'really' the story of spirit progressively realizing itself in time, but spirit, a non-natural agency, does this by using available, contingent human passions, interests, etc. This means that the first and superficial

182

(but by no means false) explanation of why Caesar crossed the Rubicon, to use Hegel's own example,[12] would refer to accidental properties of his personality and psychology, for instance his ambition. A deeper explanation would have to appeal to a number of interconnected metaphysical notions and the ways in which it was teleologically necessary that these notions be instantiated in time. The crossing of the Rubicon would be finally explained by showing why an act like that was a necessary part of the way in which self-conscious reason and spirit realized itself in history. The two explanations of the same action are for Hegel not merely compatible, but complementary.

One might think that Nietzsche's account of the slave-revolt of morality (as given in GM) had this kind of two-tiered structure. The first and superficial account of the origin of the dominant form of modern morality refers to a specific contingent historical event, the 'slave-revolt' (JGB §195, GM I. 7, 9) as a result of which a set of life-negating values gets established. The actual course of this set of events, and even, to some extent, the fact that they took place at all, is a matter of accident.[13] As Nietzsche describes it (GM I. 6f.) the slave-revolt depends on the contingent fact that a certain ruling group divides itself internally into a military faction and a priestly faction. The priestly sub-caste begins to use terms referring specifically to forms of ritual purity to differentiate itself and eventually loses out in a struggle for power with the military sub-caste. The priests decide to make common cause with the slaves, who happen to speak a language which has the grammatical distinction between subject and predicate, etc. There is nothing 'necessary' about any of this. The actual course of events and the particular form the resulting system of valuations will take will depend on such contingent conjunctions. There could, however, be (one might think, if one wanted to pursue this line of thought) a second and deeper level of analysis. At this deeper level what was 'really' happening in such seemingly accidental conjunctions was that Life was maximally affirming itself, even though the superficial form this self-affirmation took was the creation of a system of life-negating values. Much more of course, would have to be said about this, but in principle there need be nothing inconsistent in such a two-tiered theory; it would be structurally similar to Hegel's view. If Nietzsche's own views really had this structure he would just have relapsed into the kind of German metaphysics of a 'real, deep structure' partially hidden behind an apparently different surface which it was one of his major achievements to have rejected. Perhaps he does occasionally relapse, or rather he seems clearly to be relapsing all the time, but it is a not uncommon characteristic of theoretical innovators not to have full control of their own most original insights. In any case the philosophically most interesting parts of his work are those in which he undercuts two-tiered philosophies of history of the Hegelian sort. He would have been well advised to have set his face even more relentlessly than he did both against speculative philosophies of history and against the 'metaphysics of life' he inherited from Schopenhauer.

Whatever difficulties there might be about construing some of Nietzsche's pronouncements on 'Life' as compatible with his general criticism of metaphysics are compounded when one considers his doctrine of the 'will-to-power'. 'Life', it turns out, isn't, after all, the final standard. 'Life' is constantly trying to 'overcome itself', is in fact always sacrificing itself for the sake of 'power' (Z *'Von der Selbst-Überwindung'*). 'Life' is then at best a first approximation of a standard for measuring and evaluating moralities. 'Life' itself is essentially 'will-to-power' (JGB §§13, 259).

Whether or not it is a 'metaphysical' doctrine, isn't this in fact Nietzsche's final view: Certain human specimens are 'higher' than others to the extent to which they represent higher concentrations of the will-to-power? The final view would be a teleological one: The goal is the increased concentration of will-to-power. That is good which furthers this goal; that is bad which hinders it. If coercion, deception, etc. are in certain circumstances efficacious in increasing the concentration of the will-to-power, then they are to that extent good. Traditional morality is to be rejected because it now in general hinders the accumulation of will-to-power, although perhaps in the past and even in the present in some unusual circumstances it might be or might have been conducive to the growth of will-to-power.

IV

One can't miss this strand of thought in Nietzsche, that Christianity is to be rejected because it opposes the will-to-power, the vital human desire to be lord-and-master, to subordinate others to our commands and appropriate their energies, even if this requires the sacrifice of our biological existence. It is the very last part of this claim that causes difficulties. If will-to-power were very closely connected with more or less empirical biological urges, we might have a chance to determine what its content would be, what it would require in any given circumstances (e.g. self-preservation of the relevant biological entity). It seems, however, that it is just as likely, or rather even more likely, that the concentration of will-to-power will require thwarting and opposing anything we could understand as biological impulses or urges in any straightforward sense.

Perhaps the situation isn't so desperate. If will-to-power doesn't have very determinate biological content, surely it has a sufficiently clear political content. Surely people sometimes do risk various aspects of their biological well-being in order to be the ones who command, and surely this thought is sufficiently determinate to be enlightening.

Unfortunately it seems that just as the will-to-power can oppose what biology 'demands', so, too, can it find itself in direct opposition to the usual forms of political *Herrschaft*. The founding of the Second Empire in 1871 actually thwarted the

185

will-to-power of German *Geist* which had been about to claim hegemony (*'Herrschaft'* and *'Führung'*) in Europe (GT *'Versuch einer Selbstkritik'* §6; cf. GD *'Was den Deutschen abgeht'*). The 'highest specimens' may be 'commanding' figures, but the sense in which they are commanding doesn't seem to have much to do with the concentration of political power in anything like the usual sense. Goethe isn't exemplary by virtue of anything having to do with his position or activity at the Court in Weimar.

What seems more important in the case of many of the instances Nietzsche cites and discusses when he speaks of 'highest specimens' is that they are in some way admirable. Goethe is an instance of an especially high degree of human flourishing not because he is (politically) powerful, but because his life and works arouse admiration. Of course the fact that he arouses admiration may in fact increase his power in that others may follow his lead, do as he suggests (or commands) etc. but to look at Goethe from the perspective of human flourishing is to look at what in him and his work inspires admiration, not at his political power. Sometimes, to be sure, what inspires admiration may be the way military or political power is acquired or wielded, as in the case of Napoleon (whom Nietzsche seems to have admired), but military and political power alone won't necessarily be high on the scale of concentration of will-to-power. The Second Empire has political and military power in abundance, but isn't admirable, and Nietzsche is as opposed to it as he is to Christianity.

This position may seem counterintuitive because the strong impression many readers have is that one of Nietzsche's basic claims is that finally only power (in something like our everyday sense of that term) is truly admirable. I'm suggesting that when Nietzsche is at his most interesting he doesn't think that admiration is locked onto power (in the usual sense) as its object, and admiration is what is finally important for him (cf. GM I. 12). 'Will-to-power' is an empty, metaphysical concept.

Being vital, flourishing, being a 'higher specimen' means being able to inspire admiration. There seems also to be no single substantive trait which *all* higher specimens have in common by virtue of which they succeed in getting themselves admired; they are admired in different ways for different traits.

Admiration (*Bewunderung*) and its opposite, disgust (*Ekel*), are for Nietzsche two of the most powerful internal forces that move human beings (JGB §26; GM I. 11, II. 24, III. 14 etc.).[14] Both admiration and disgust in the first instance are elicited by and directed at concrete, individual objects, persons, or situations, and what will be an object of admiration or of disgust varies from person to person and from time to time. In a sense the most important fact about a given person for Nietzsche is which particular objects (or people) that person finds admirable (at what time), and which disgusting, and why. There are no naturally or antecedently fixed criteria of what is worthy of admiration. It doesn't follow from this that no generalizations whatever are possible about what sorts of things a given person or group of people tends to admire, but such generalizations can at best be only first approximations or crude rules of thumb. Extreme uniformity, consistency, and predictability of admiration may occur, but if it does, it doesn't indicate convergence to correct perception of some objective properties, but rather is more likely to signify that some extraneous social pressure is operating – usually this means that some dominant group is enforcing uniformity in order to maintain its own position (cf. ÜWL) – or that one is looking at an especially unperceptive group of particularly boring people, deadbeats unable to respond to anything novel or to reevaluate what they already know.

Although there are no 'objective' properties of people, actions, and things by virtue of which they are inherently worthy of being admired, it is also not the case that I (or, we) can simply *decide* (in the usual sense of 'decide') what things we will now admire. To say that a higher specimen is something that succeeds in getting itself admired is to say that I (or, you, or, we) *really do* admire it, not just that we say we do, or even that we try assiduously to admire it, although it is also the case that sometimes (but not always) trying hard enough will eventually enable me to admire something I may originally have been indifferent to, or only pretended to admire. Just as one can't really live the life of a Bronze Age chief, a samurai, or a Teutonic Knight in 1990s Western Europe[15] (although perhaps one can admire some of the traits such people exhibited), so equally whether or not one can really admire certain people or acts will depend on a variety of factors, some having to do with external circumstances and some with my own existing habits, reactions, personality traits, projects, etc. My own reactions of admiration or disgust won't either be a simple deterministic product of natural and social forces – because I can influence them to some extent – nor will they be something I can simply turn on and off *ad libitum*. Again the Christian sharp dichotomy 'determined/free' is, Nietzsche thinks, useless or rather counterproductive in trying to allow us to get a firm conceptual grasp on this topic. The extent to which an individual person will be able to reform, control, or redirect his or her admiration or disgust will itself vary; people of strong character ('will') will in general be more able to do this than others will (JGB §284; GM III. 12).

One way, then, to think about what we commonly call a 'morality' is as a set of forms of admiration and disgust congealed into socially established catalogues of 'oughts' and 'ought nots'. Nietzsche's account of the 'ought' in question here proceeds in successive stages, like the gradual unpeeling of an onion, and it is important not to confuse the stages. For purposes of simplicity of exposition I will distinguish three such stages.

First, for most people in nineteenth-century Europe Christianity or one of its derivatives is a central element in their morality; for such Christians and post-Christians the important

188

'oughts' form a catalogue of the appropriate virtues and vices for the members of a universal mutual-aid society of slaves. We 'ought' to admire those who would be good members of such a society and feel disgust at those who would not. Nietzsche subjects this moralizing Christian 'ought' to a number of criticisms, some of which have been canvassed earlier in this essay.

In the second place there are 'free spirits' who have distanced themselves in varying degrees from the Christian insistencies of 'morality' but who may still feel the bite of some elements originally derived from the Christian synthesis (cf. FW §344). Thus in the *'Vorrede'* to M Nietzsche describes himself as still standing under the domination of the (originally Christian) virtue of 'truthfulness' and its associated 'oughts'; he still thinks that one ought to strive to find out the final truth about the world and face up to it. Something like a 'morality' with its own kind of *'Verbindlichkeit'* is possible here among free spirits, although a highly individualistic one in which the virtues of social cooperation will have perhaps a fragile and uncertain standing. Truthful admiration (or disgust) could give rise to various 'oughts' such as that I ought to emulate what I truthfully admire (i.e. what I find I really admire when I have found out the truth about it).

Finally, however, and this is the third of the stages of Nietzsche's discussion, if one takes 'truthfulness' to its limit, one will gradually lose one's hold on what 'ought' could conceivably mean at all, what non-illusory sense it might have for anyone to think that something 'ought' to be the case which in fact is not. Seen from a sufficiently non-anthropocentric perspective – from the view-point of the most radical 'truthfulness' – the world is just what it is, a huge, historically and spatially extended brute fact. In fact, 'up there where the air is clear' it might start to become increasingly difficult to think that there was any real *point* in being truthful at all (GD *'Moral als Widernatur'* §6; WM §§15, 36, 598, 602 etc.). This position, which Nietzsche sometimes calls 'nihilism' (WM §598) isn't comfortably inhabitable by an individual human being in the long run. Nietzsche thinks, however, that such nihilism may be the fate of contemporary society. Since human cognitive capacities are social developments of biological phenomena, not sparks of the Divine Fire, there isn't any reason to assume *a priori* that the concepts and theories we are capable of coming up with will be coherent, consistent, and fully determinate, or that they will have clear application at all far beyond what is needed for our direct survival and our normal social life (WM §§494, 602). Beyond these limits we should rather expect our thinking and valuing to lose their determinacy. It isn't at all clear whether or not this last thought is consoling or further demoralizing, and that in itself is probably for Nietzsche a further sign of our weakness.

v

This would seem, then, to leave one with a very anarchic doctrine. Many varieties of human types and individuals exist. Some are admirable (i.e. admired by some people at some times); others disgusting. If you are the kind of person with a refined capacity for admiration and disgust you will probably find yourself drawn by your admiration for certain paradigmatic exemplars of particular properties to act in certain ways which may make you in turn an object of admiration. To be admirable is always to be admired *by* someone, whether that be God, the gods, other people, or oneself.

Although the doctrine is anarchic, the world it describes need not be completely chaotic. In this world of shifting forms of admiration and disgust a 'better' and 'worse' can be distinguished in that I can succeed in my projects and enterprises and that is more admirable to those who endorse those projects than failure would be. Of course, what I call 'success' others may call 'failure' because they define the project differently. What for the Romans is 'failure' (e.g. the crucifixion and death of Jesus) can be 'success' for Christians. There is no set of projects that has automatic standing for *all* humans, and contains within itself its own irrefutable answer to the question: 'Why try to do that?' That does not imply, of course, that certain forms of this question might not have irrefutable answers for particular people. Luther, perhaps, really could do no other. Not even self-preservation is a project that is automatically self-validating for all; martyrdom is not an inherently incoherent project.[16]

In the final analysis there is just the mass of human individuals and groups exercising power or being dominated, succeeding or failing at various projects, and, at a slightly eccentric angle to this world of direct action, a flux of admiration of various things by various people and of disgust at various things by various people who have or have not tried and have or have not succeeded in influencing their own reactions of admiration and disgust. This gives rise to a wide variety of different 'oughts' of different forces and imports. There is no neutral external point from which any one of these 'oughts' could be incontrovertibly 'grounded'. In one sense this is a very important fact indeed – one is tempted to say that it is the most important fact there is for the servile philosopher in search of 'the unconditioned' – but it is also in another sense of little real significance practically. We live in a world in which we are abundantly supplied with 'oughts' and we have, and are in fact to some extent in the grip of, our own reactions of disgust and admiration. These won't disappear. Just thinking about them differently won't change them. To modify them would require a long and complex process with an uncertain outcome. I may try to learn to admire what people I admire value; I may or may not succeed. My (and, our) reactions of admiration and disgust may motivate us to try to ensure that certain objects of admiration (including perhaps certain admirable ways of being) attain a more stable existence, or that the conditions for the emergence of such objects and ways of being are made as propitious as possible. We may also be motivated to try to prevent disgusting forms of life and action. Part of the way in which we might go about doing this is by enforcing through public, institutionalized sanctions certain ways of behaving; we might even hope eventually to succeed in causing those around us to internalize certain ways of feeling, reacting, evaluating, and thinking. Especially in cases in which a certain group of people succeeds in imposing such a set of predictable ways of acting and evaluating (oriented toward the production of admired 'objects' and the suppression of disgusting 'objects' and forms of behaviour) not just on others but also on themselves, we will be likely to speak of a paradigmatic case of a 'morality'.

These more or less systematized forms of feeling and judging possess *'Verbindlichkeit'* to the extent to which they are socially enforced, or to the extent to which they arise out of a complex history in which physiological facts, forms of social pressure, and individual efforts have interacted to produce a state in which they actually have a hold on people, or to the extent to which they really are necessary or highly useful for the generation and preservation of particular kinds of admired human types or individuals (JGB §§188, 262). If Venice (i.e. 'Venice' as a social and cultural enterprise, matrix for the production of admired human individuals and works of art, perhaps itself an object of identification and esteem) is not to fall into decadence, the waters in the canals must be controlled, but also *this* set of customs, this form of evaluating, feeling, and willing may be necessary and thus *'verbindlich'*. If the demands of controlling the level of water in the canals and of admired forms of living conflict, it isn't obvious, or, Nietzsche thinks, obviously good that the demands of sanitation win out.

Any morality will represent only one choice among a potentially infinite plurality of possible objects of admiration, although it won't be a 'choice' any individual human being makes *ad libitum;* as such it will always float over a lagoon of anarchic, partially unstructured acts of individual admiration

192

and disgust. A morality is one way of regimenting the multi-plicitous florescence of human growth among others (GD *'Moral als Widernatur'* §6; JGB §§188, 199, 262) and has no 'ground' beyond historical inertia and the fact that it is (or can effectively claim to be) necessary (or overwhelmingly benefi-cial) for the survival and production of certain admired human types. Realizing this with complete clarity won't in itself neces-sarily undermine the *'Verbindlichkeit'* of the morality in ques-tion. If, of course, one turns away from a historically given admired type with disgust or indifference, or if the morality for whatever reason ceases to be necessary for the production of the admired type, then the morality will lose its *'Verbind-lichkeit'*.

Philosophers, Nietzsche thinks, are to be law-givers and commanders (*'Befehlende und Gesetzgeber'* JGB §211). Their task will be to 'create new values', new forms and objects of admira-tion, and to help elaborate the kinds of socially anchored feel-ings, beliefs, and forms of living and evaluating which will form the horizon within which such new values are most likely to be realized. This will require coercion because few admirable things arise completely spontaneously (JGB §§188, 199). The philosopher will realize that the resulting morality is a human invention, a *'Schein'*, a dream, if you will, resting ultimately only on the highly variable forms of human admiration; nevertheless the appropriate attitude toward the new morality will be the one described by Nietzsche in GT when speaking of Apollonian art: *'Es ist ein Traum; ich will ihn weiter träumen.'* (GT §1)[17]

NOTES

1  I don't mean *'Sittlichkeit'* in Hegel's technical sense, but just in the ordinary everyday sense of the word in German.
2  Strictly speaking, Nietzsche says that people have in the past under-stood themselves as essentially valuating animals (GM II. 8), and he asks whether this isn't the case (*'Ist Leben nicht Abschätzen . . .'*? JGB

§9) so it isn't completely unproblematic to attribute to Nietzsche the view that all human life involves valuation. This need not be incompatible with anti-essentialism. If one really does think that there is no firm and strict distinction between literal and metaphorical speech, one can allow oneself to use forms of speech that might look at first glance very much like those found in traditional, essentialist metaphysics, while treating the claims in question as mere '*Annahmen bis auf weiteres*' (WM §497). Valuation or discrimination is also only *one* component of what Christians and post-Christians in the nineteenth century would call a 'morality' because they will wish to distinguish (purportedly) specifically moral forms of valuation from other kinds.

3 There is a seventh thesis which is an exceedingly important constituent of Christianity according to Nietzsche, but which doesn't play much of a direct role in the forms of morality that derive from Christianity in the nineteenth century, namely:

(7*) Suffering results from sin (M §78; GM III. 15).

There are, of course, forms of morality, even nineteenth-century ones that don't fit at all well into this schema, e.g. utilitarianism (if one considers that a form of 'morality'). Most utilitarians would have rejected at least thesis (4) above.

4 Nietzsche rejects both the view that the prescriptions of morality should apply equally to all, and that proper moral evaluations should be such that anyone could in principle agree to them.

5 The 'slave revolt' of morality (JGB §195; GM I. 7) was a historically unique event, and did not succeed in creating new 'positive' values, but only 'reactive' ones (GM I. 10).

6 Nietzsche uses the phrase 'create values' both in the sense of inventing new kinds of values or conceptions of value and in the sense of creating new objects of value.

7 Unfortunately Nietzsche never discusses in detail the relation between his doctrine of the 'pathos of distance' (as the origin of value) and the distinction between 'active' and 'reactive' forms of willing (discussed in GM I. 10). Obviously Nietzsche must think that aristocratic valuations that arise from this 'pathos of distance' are 'active' not 'reactive' (although they in some sense require the existence of the slaves as objects of contempt), but how exactly this is to be understood is not completely clear. Deleuze (1962) sees the problem and suggests that 'active/reactive' and 'yea-saying/nay-saying' are two separate distinctions. That seems right, but I fail to see how it solves the difficulty.

8  Since this point is often misunderstood, let me repeat it in a slightly different form. When Nietzsche denies that the will is free, this is not best understood as like the denial: 'The tomato is not poisonous (because it is edible, i.e. non-poisonous)', but rather as like the denial I would express if I were to say in a society which divides all days of the week into 'lucky' and 'unlucky' days: 'Friday is not an unlucky day (because the whole contrast 'lucky/unlucky' has no useful application to days of the week)'.

9  Oddly enough Nietzsche thinks that this notion of exchange of equivalents in commercial transactions is older than even the most rudimentary forms of social organization (GM II. 8).

10  Nietzsche distinguishes two stages in the genesis of 'bad conscience'. First there is a process of 'internalization' (GM II. 16): Instead of fear that I will suffer at the hands of another because I have failed to repay an external debt, I begin to make myself suffer because of failure to repay some 'internal debt', i.e. failure to obey the dictates of the morality traditional in my society. Then this need to punish can be 'moralized' (GM II. 21; III. 20) by being supplied with the categories of 'evil', 'sin', etc. When my bad conscience has been 'moralized' I won't just try to punish myself for non-traditional behaviour, but I will feel myself to be 'evil', 'sinful', 'guilty' etc.

11  At WM §4 Nietzsche analyses some of the strengths and advantages of Christian morality.

12  Hegel (1970), p. 45ff.

13  Nietzsche's view here is like the one I ascribe to him about free will/determinism. It isn't so much that he thinks historical events are 'contingent' in some positive sense, but that the distinction 'contingent/necessary' is useless in the study of history. Since nineteenth-century philosophers of history stress 'necessity' it is convenient in exposition to emphasize 'contingency' but actually I think Nietzsche would prefer to avoid the distinction altogether.

14  Actually 'admiration' seems to have a second opposite, 'contempt' (*Verachtung*). I can't here pursue the analysis of admiration, contempt, and disgust in Nietzsche, but I think this would in principle be well worth doing.

15  Cf. Williams (1985), pp. 160ff.

16  Although there are some striking similarities between Nietzsche's views and those of Hobbes, there are also two important differences. First, Nietzsche denies that self-preservation should be central to our thinking about human life. Biological self-pres-

ervation is not an overriding concern for humans. Rather, Nietzsche holds, significant numbers of humans are willing to put their lives at risk for the sake of leading what they would think to be a *worthwhile* life (JGB §13; cf. GM III. 1, 28). Nowadays we associate this kind of view with Hegel (cf. Siep [1974]), but it was common enough in Germany in the nineteenth century. Nietzsche had notoriously little interest in or knowledge of Hegel, so it is unlikely that there is any direct influence here. Second, Nietzsche would have no truck with anything like Hobbes' conception of a 'law of nature'. As a 'Precept, or general Rule, found out by Reason' (Hobbes [1996], chapter XIV) a 'law of nature' would fall afoul of Nietzsche's general criticism of conceptions of 'reason'.

17 I have benefitted from comments on a previous draft of this essay by Michael Forster (University of Chicago), Michael Hardimon (University of California at San Diego), Susan James (Girton College, Cambridge), Pierre Keller (University of California at Riverside), Susanna Mitchell (Lucy Cavendish College, Cambridge), Fred Neuhouser (University of California at San Diego), Onora O'Neill (Newnham College, Cambridge), and Quentin Skinner (Christ's College, Cambridge).

REFERENCES

Works by Nietzsche are cited according to the Colli-Montinari edition (Nietzsche 1980) except for WM, which is cited according to the sections of the old Gast edition (Nietzsche 1901). The following abbreviations are used for works by Nietzsche (with volume and page references to the Colli-Montinari edition in round brackets):

EH   = *Ecce Homo* (Nietzsche 1980, vol. 6, pp. 257ff.)
FW   = *The Gay Science* (Nietzsche 1980, vol. 3, pp. 345ff.)
GD   = *The Twilight of Idols* (Nietzsche 1980, vol. 6, pp. 57ff.)
GM   = *The Genealogy of Morality* (Nietzsche 1980, vol. 5, pp. 247ff.)
GS   = 'The Greek State' (Nietzsche 1980, vol. 1, pp. 764ff.)
GT   = *The Birth of Tragedy* (Nietzsche 1980, vol. 1, pp. 11ff.)
JGB  = *Beyond Good and Evil* (Nietzsche 1980, vol. 5, pp. 11ff.)
M    = *Daybreak* (Nietzsche 1980, vol. 3, pp. 11ff.)
NNH  = 'The Use and Abuse of History for Life' (Nietzsche 1980, vol. 1, pp. 245ff.)
ÜWL  = 'On Truth and Lie in an Extra-moral Sense' (Nietzsche 1980, vol. 1, pp. 875ff.)

WM = *The Will to Power* (cited according to Nietzsche 1901)
Z = *Thus Spake Zarathustra* (Nietzsche 1980, vol. 4, pp. 11ff.)

Deleuze, G. (1962), *Nietzsche et la philosophie.* Paris: Presses Universitaires de France.

Hegel, G. W. F. (1970), *Vorlesungen über die Philosophie der Geschichte* in *Werke in zwanzig Bänden,* Moldenhauer and Michel (eds.). Frankfurt/M.: Suhrkamp, vol. 12.

Hobbes, T. (1996), *Leviathan,* Richard Tuck, Cambridge: Cambridge University Press.

Nietzsche, F. (1901), *Der Wille zur Macht: Versuch einer Umwertung aller Werte,* ausgewählt und geordnet von Peter Gast unter Mitwirkung von Elisabeth Förster-Nietzsche. Stuttgart: Kröner.

Nietzsche, F. (1980), *Sämtliche Werke: Kritische Studienausgabe in 15 Bänden,* ed. G. Colli and M. Montinari. Berlin: Walter de Gruyter.

Siep, L. (1974), '*Der Kampf um Anerkennung: Zu Hegels Auseinandersetzung mit Hobbes in den Jenaer Schriften*' in *Hegel-Studien* 9.

Williams, B. (1985), *Ethics and the Limits of Philosophy.* Cambridge, Mass.: Harvard University Press.

# INDEX

# Index

# Index

# Index